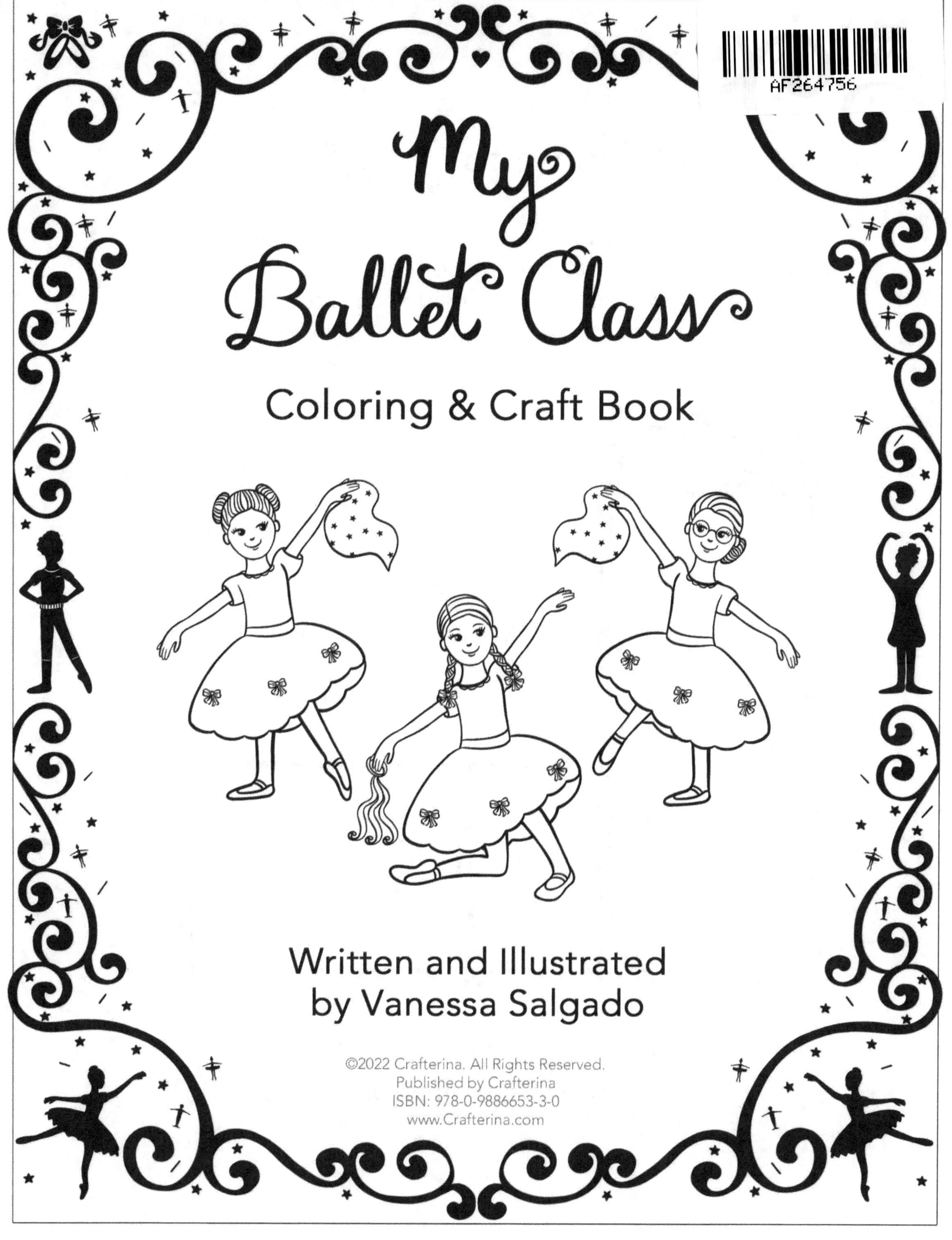

# My Ballet Class

## Coloring & Craft Book

Written and Illustrated
by Vanessa Salgado

©2022 Crafterina. All Rights Reserved.
Published by Crafterina
ISBN: 978-0-9886653-3-0
www.Crafterina.com

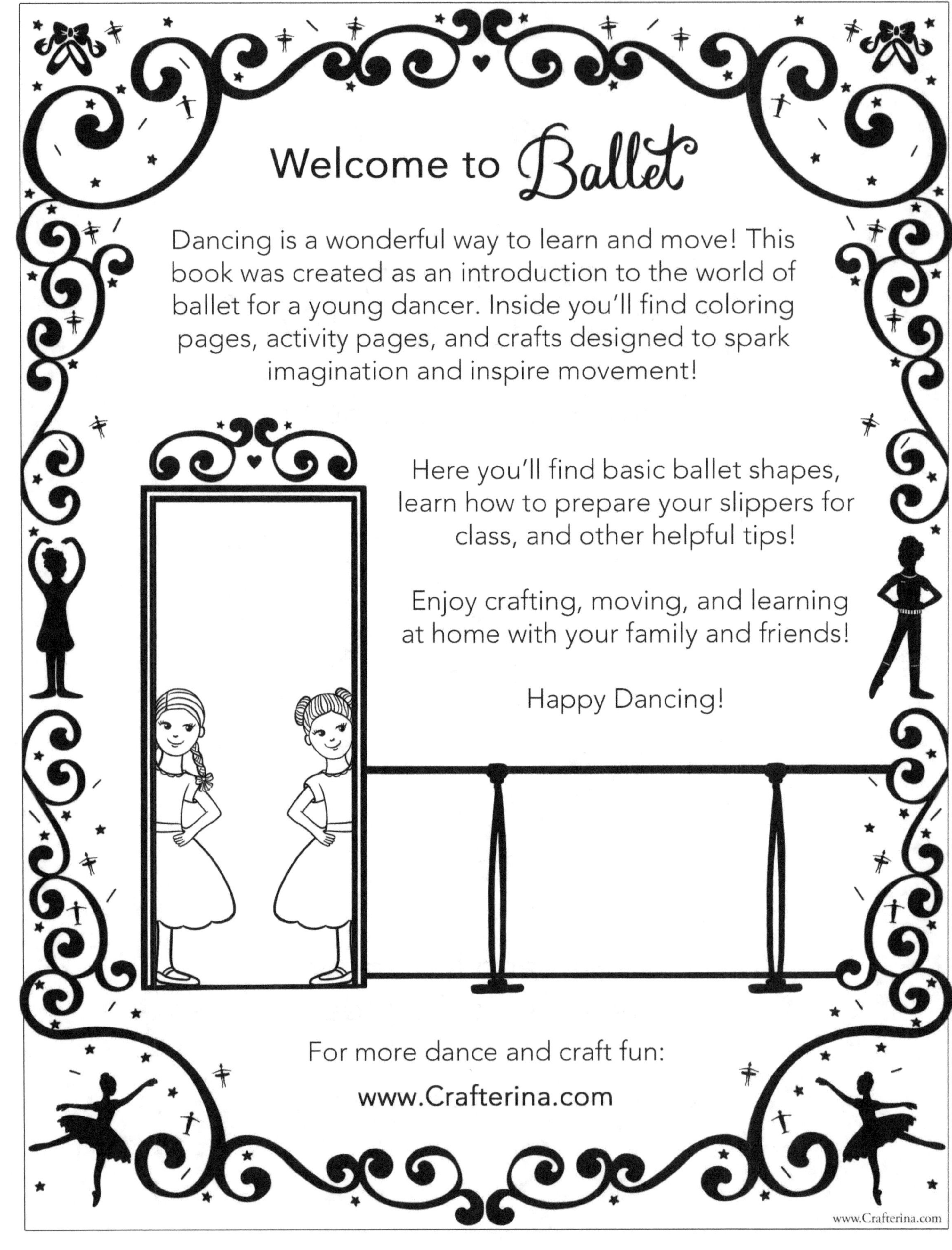

# Welcome to *Ballet*

Dancing is a wonderful way to learn and move! This book was created as an introduction to the world of ballet for a young dancer. Inside you'll find coloring pages, activity pages, and crafts designed to spark imagination and inspire movement!

Here you'll find basic ballet shapes, learn how to prepare your slippers for class, and other helpful tips!

Enjoy crafting, moving, and learning at home with your family and friends!

Happy Dancing!

For more dance and craft fun:

www.Crafterina.com

# Welcome to *Ballet*

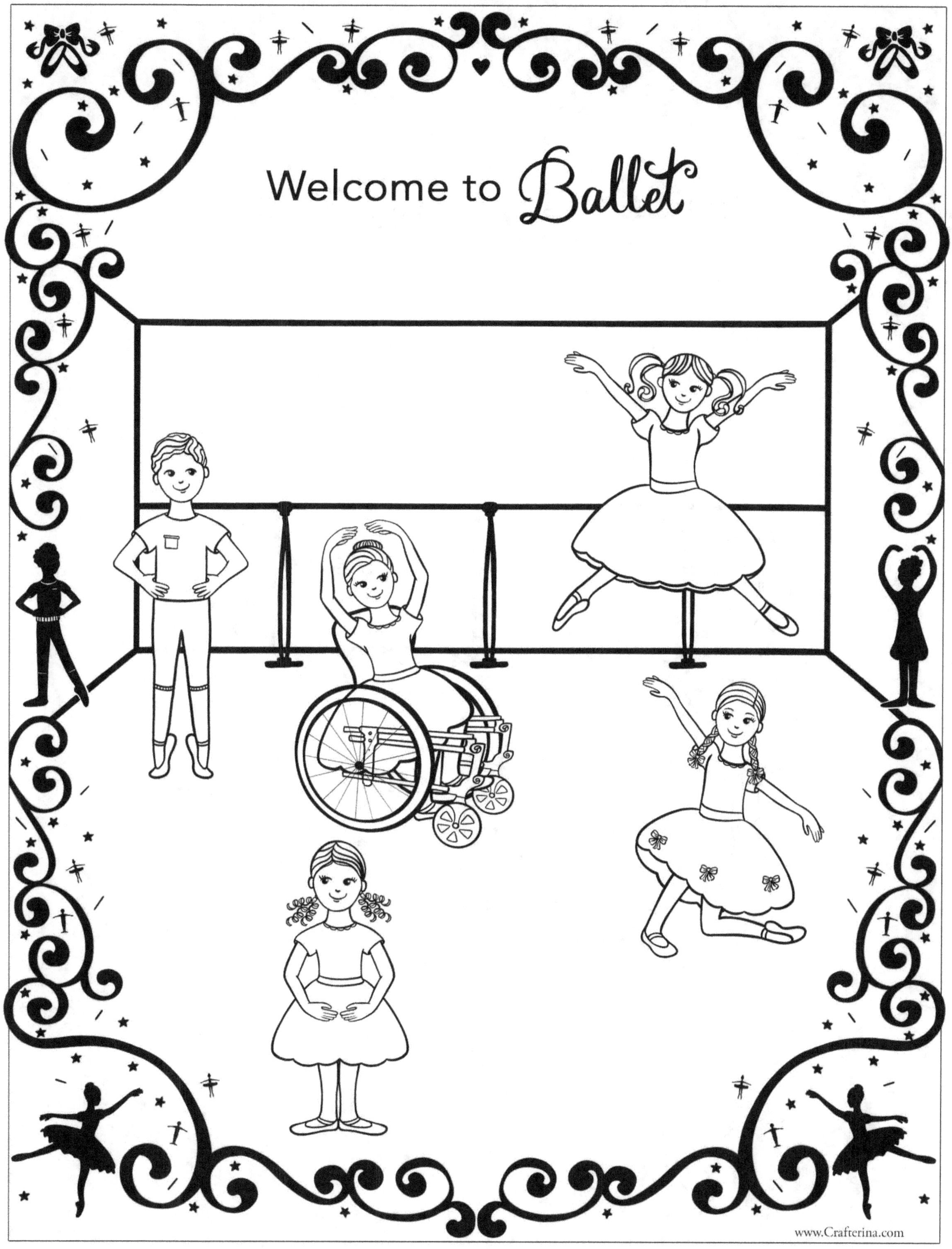

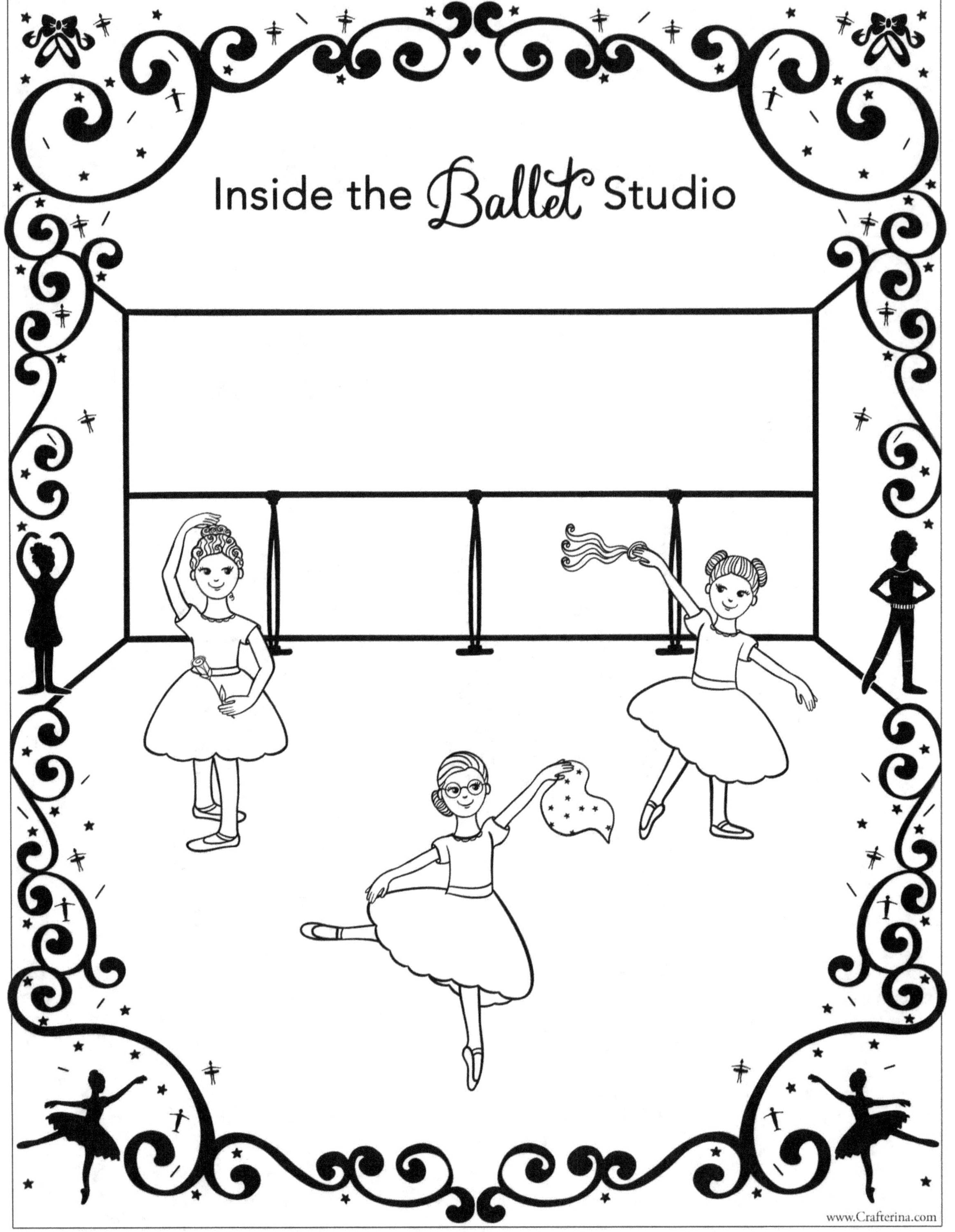

Inside the Ballet Studio
www.Crafterina.com

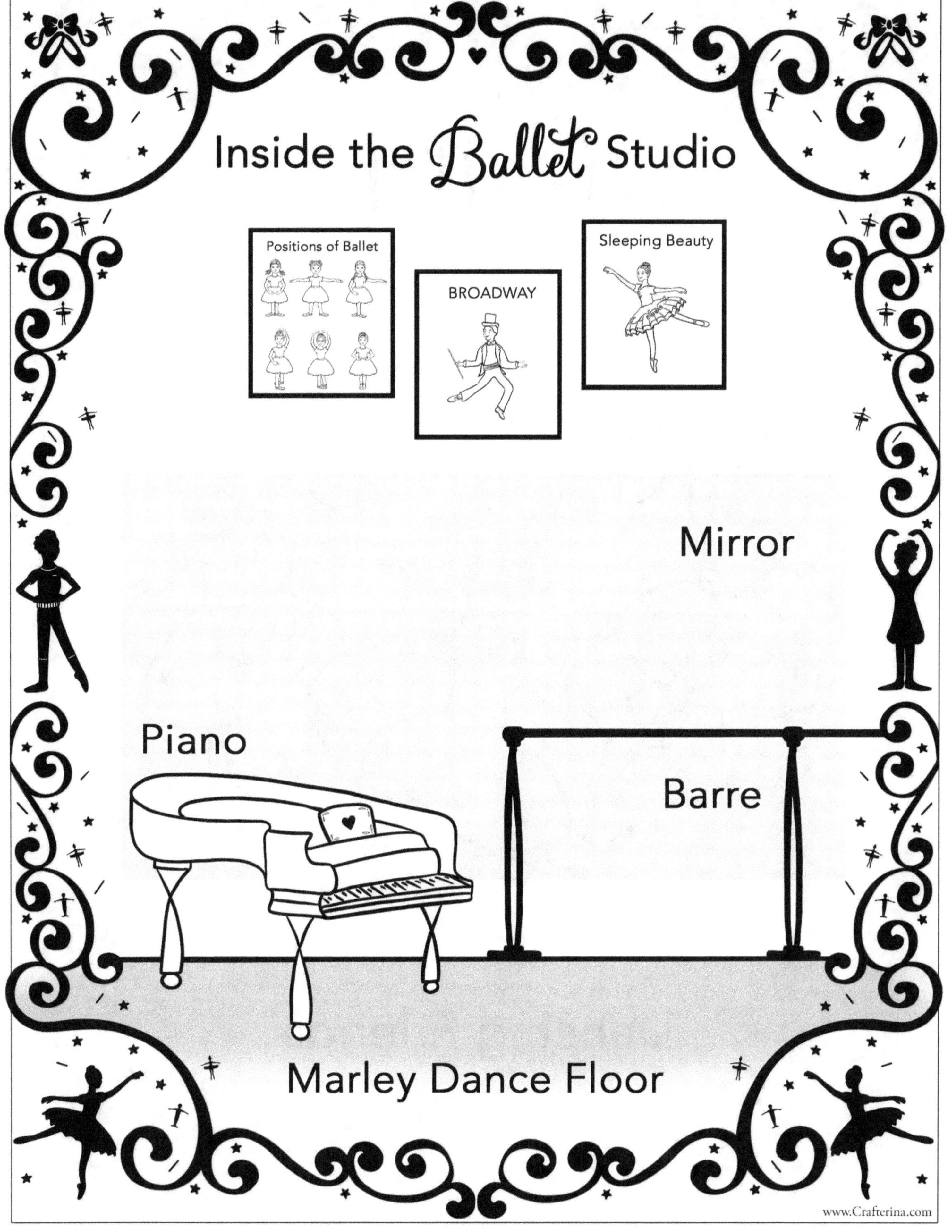

Inside the Ballet Studio
Positions of Ballet
BROADWAY
Sleeping Beauty
Mirror
Piano
Barre
Marley Dance Floor
www.Crafterina.com

# Ballet

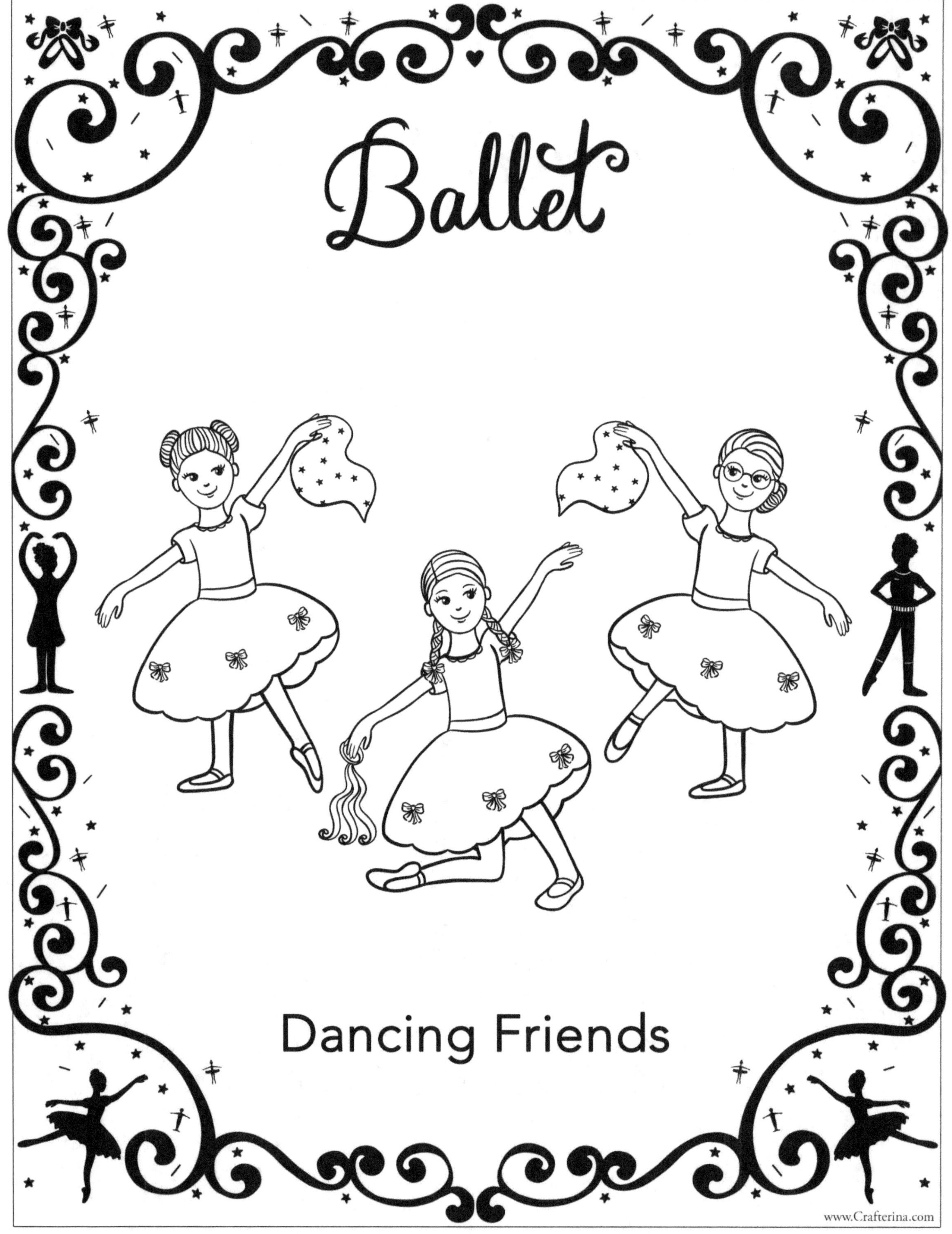

Dancing Friends

# Ballet

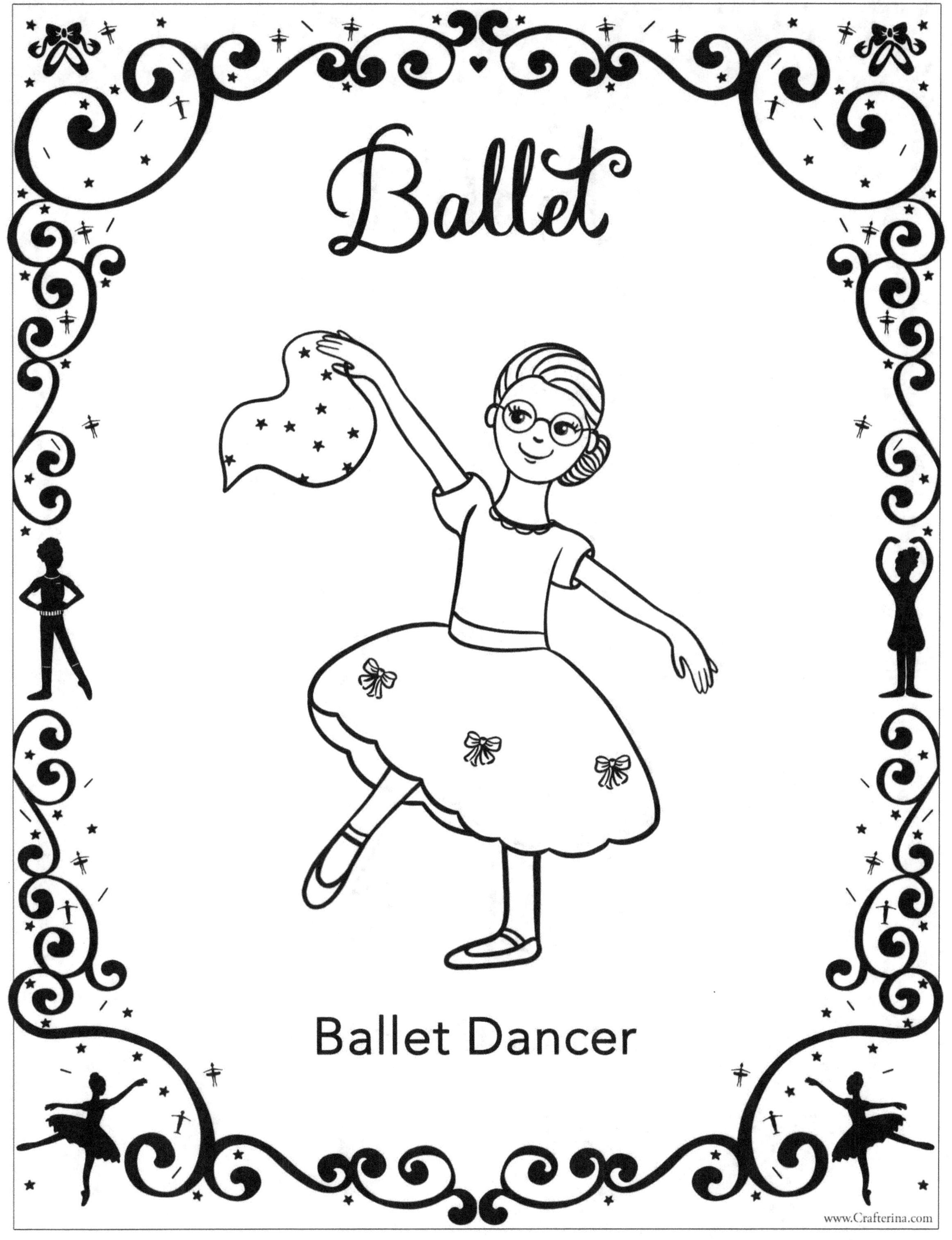

**Ballet Dancer**

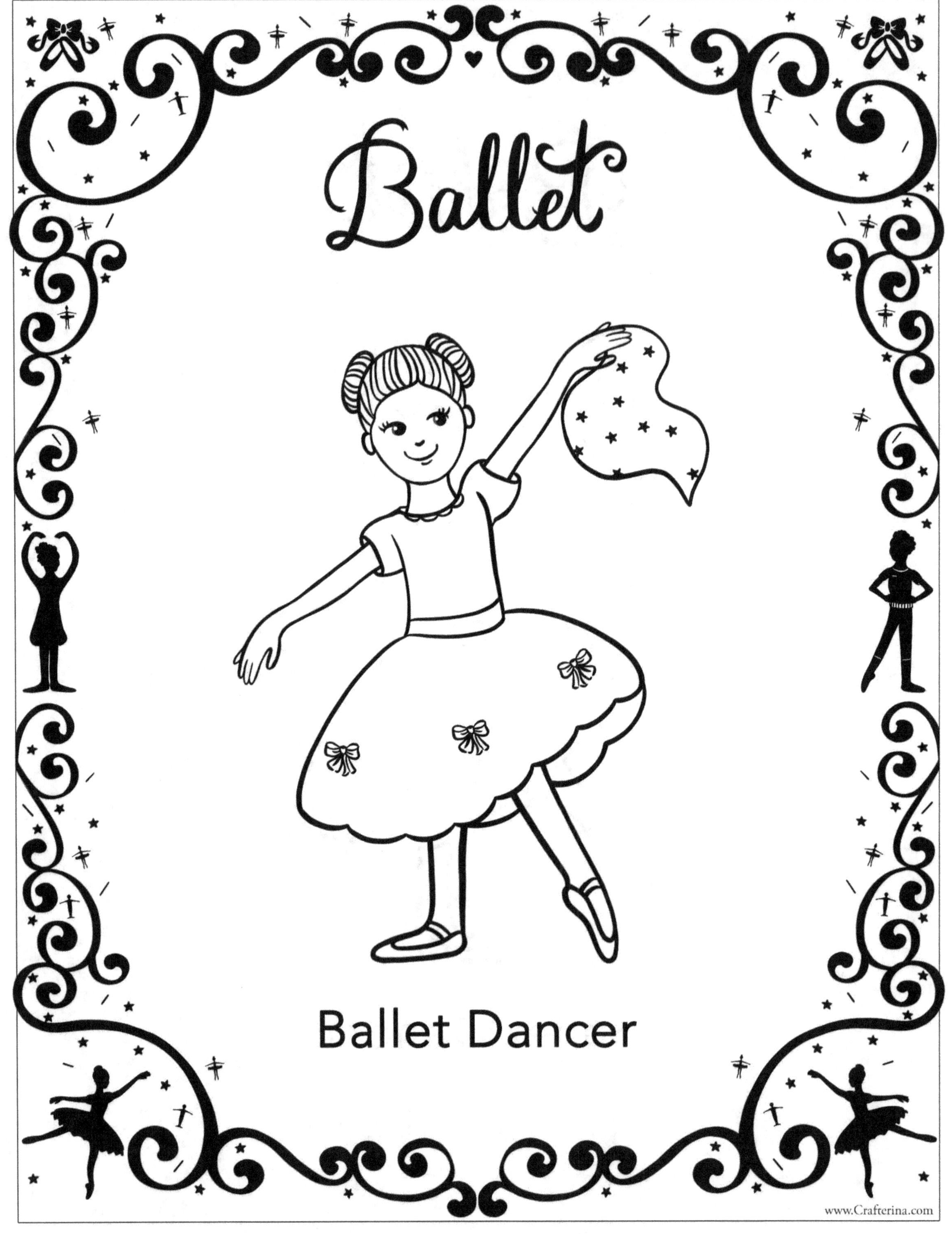

Ballet
Ballet Dancer
www.Crafterina.com

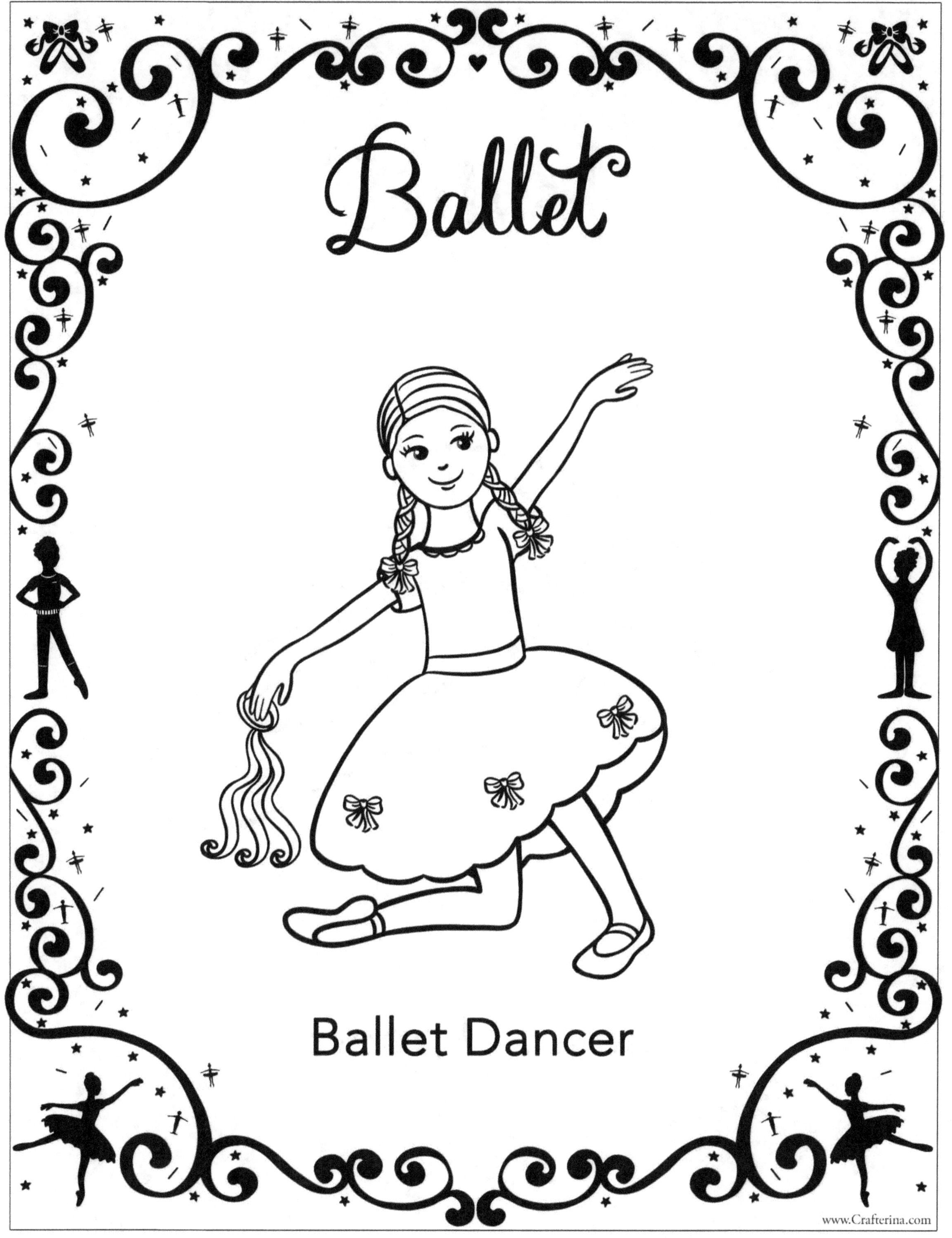

Ballet
Ballet Dancer
www.Crafterina.com

# Ballet

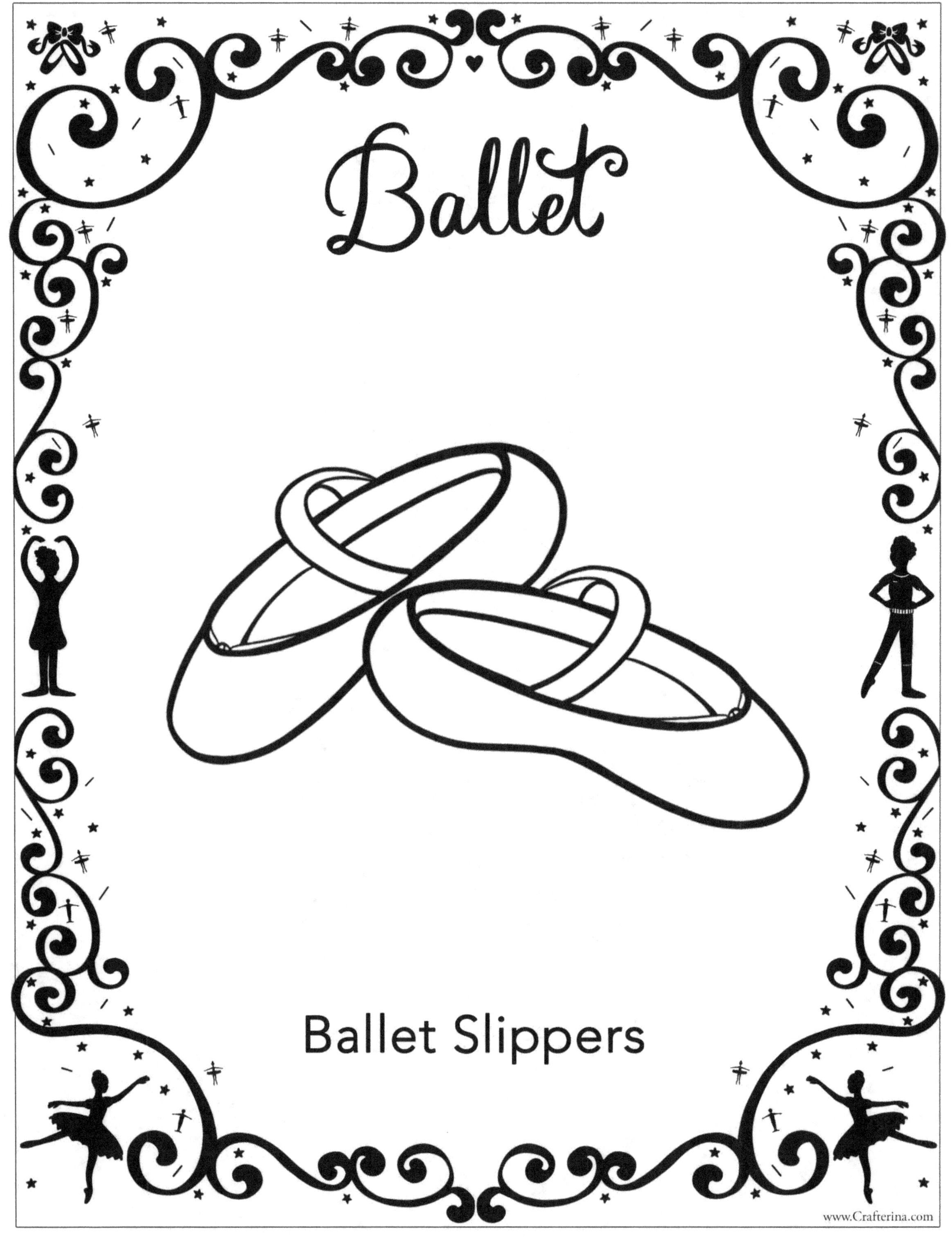

## Ballet Slippers

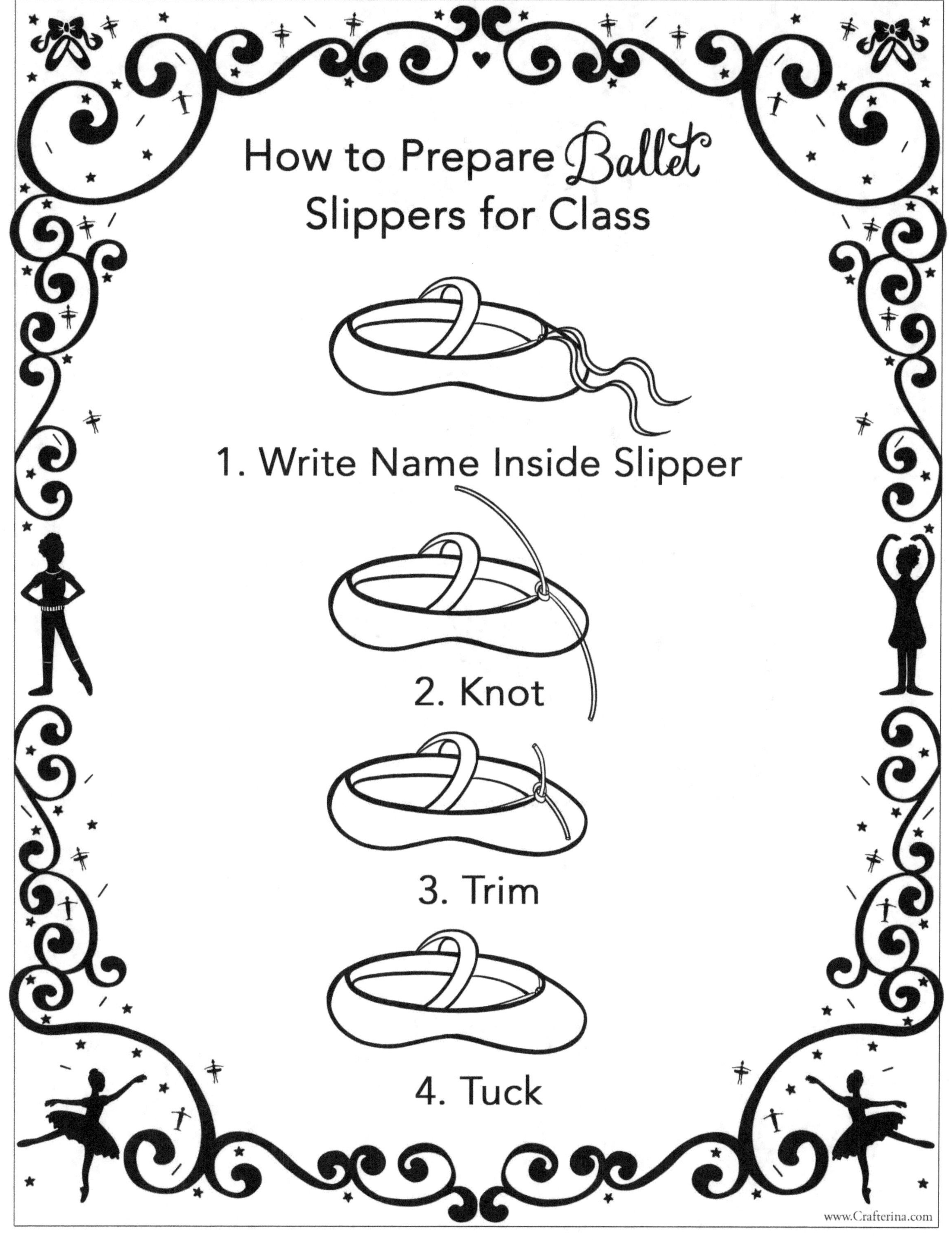

How to Prepare Ballet Slippers for Class
1. Write Name Inside Slipper
2. Knot
3. Trim
4. Tuck
www.Crafterina.com

# Ballet

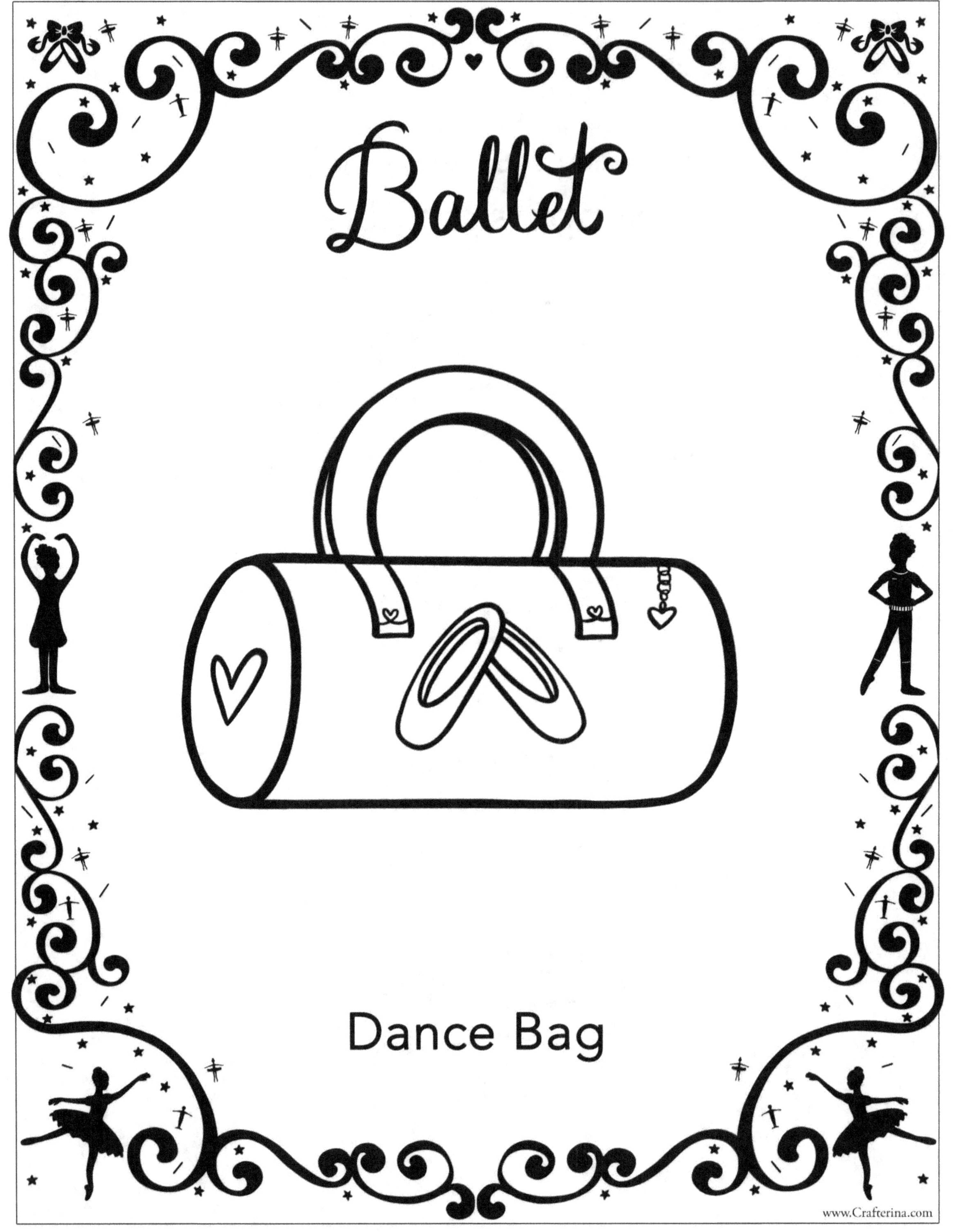

Dance Bag

# Inside My *Ballet* Bag

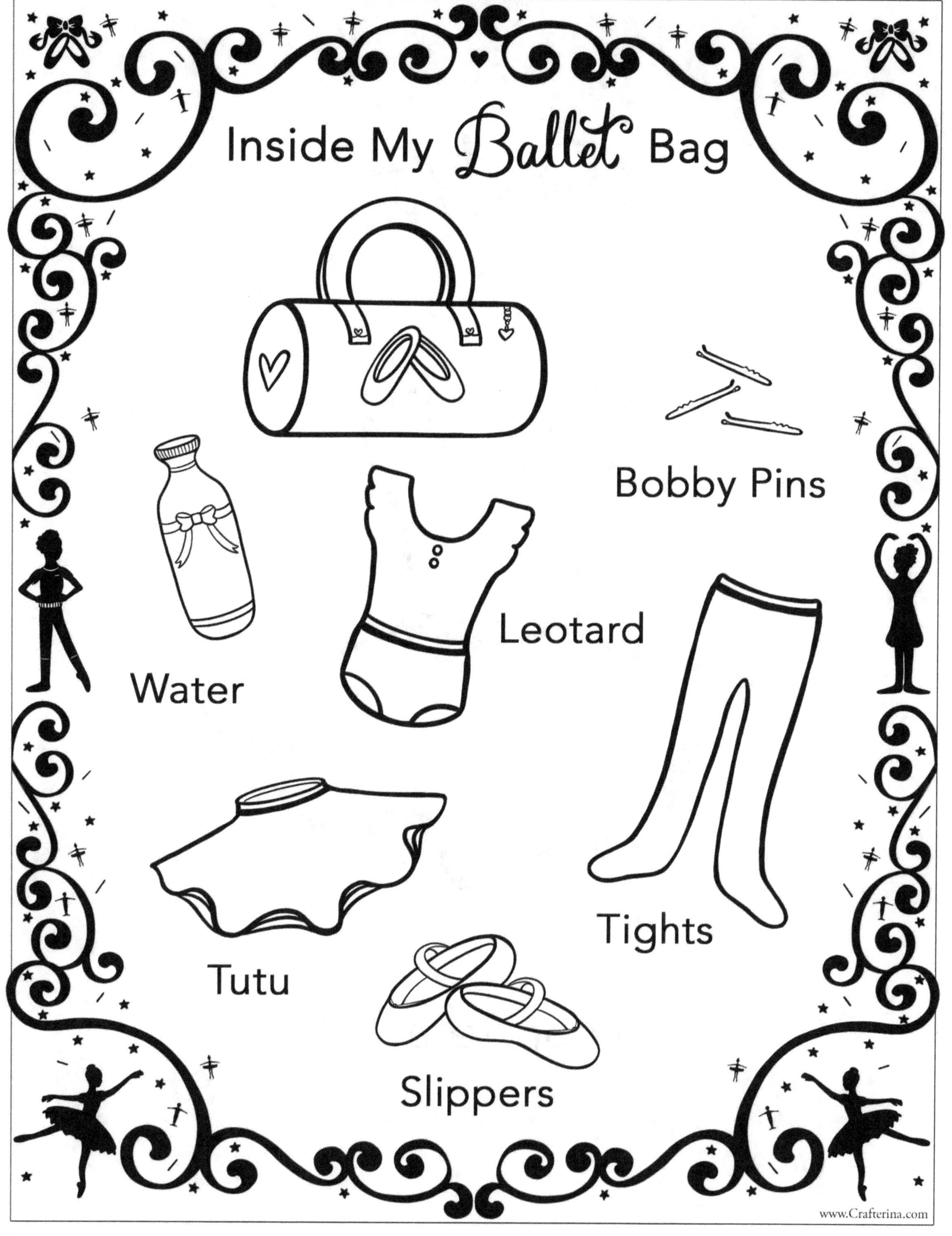

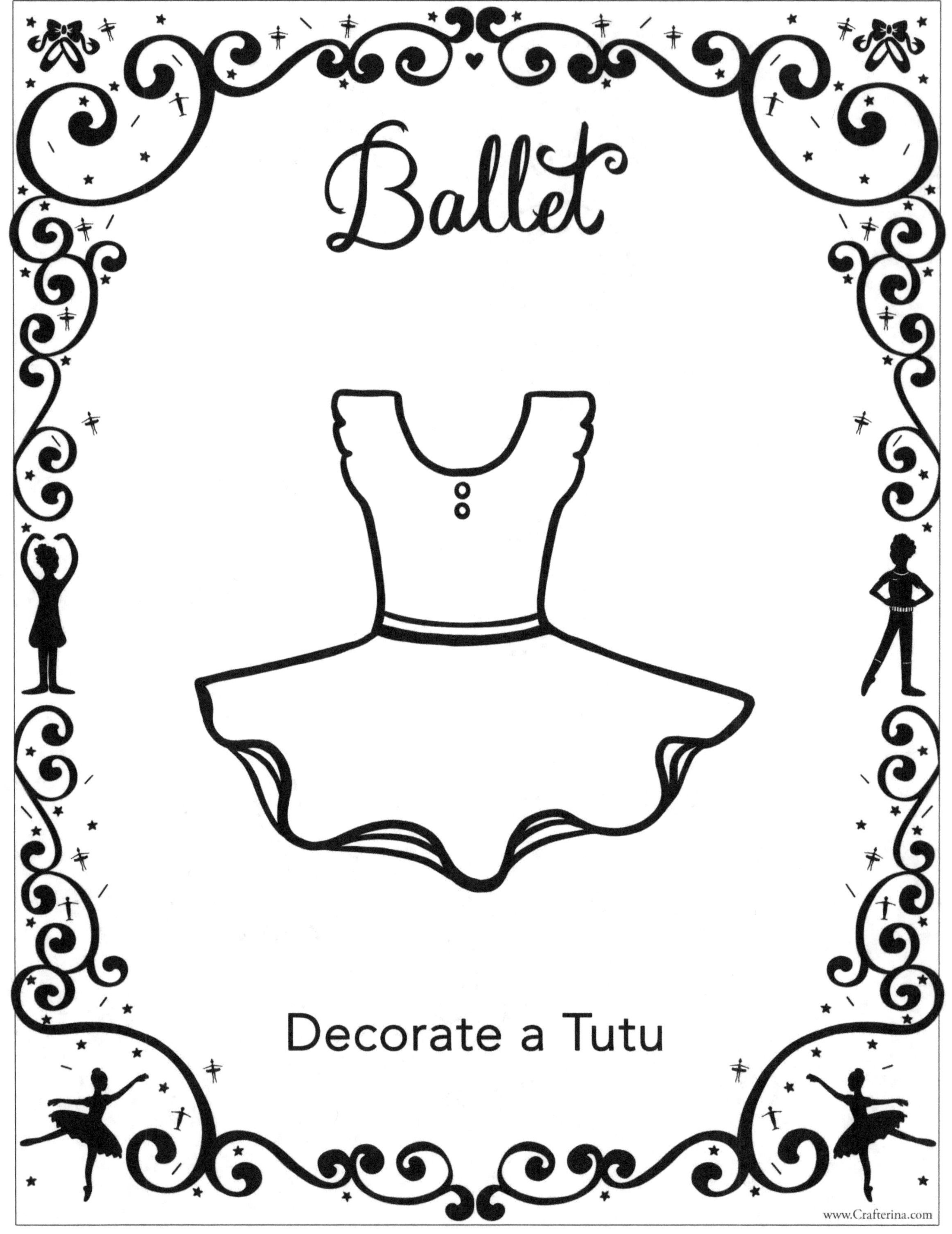
Ballet
Decorate a Tutu
www.Crafterina.com

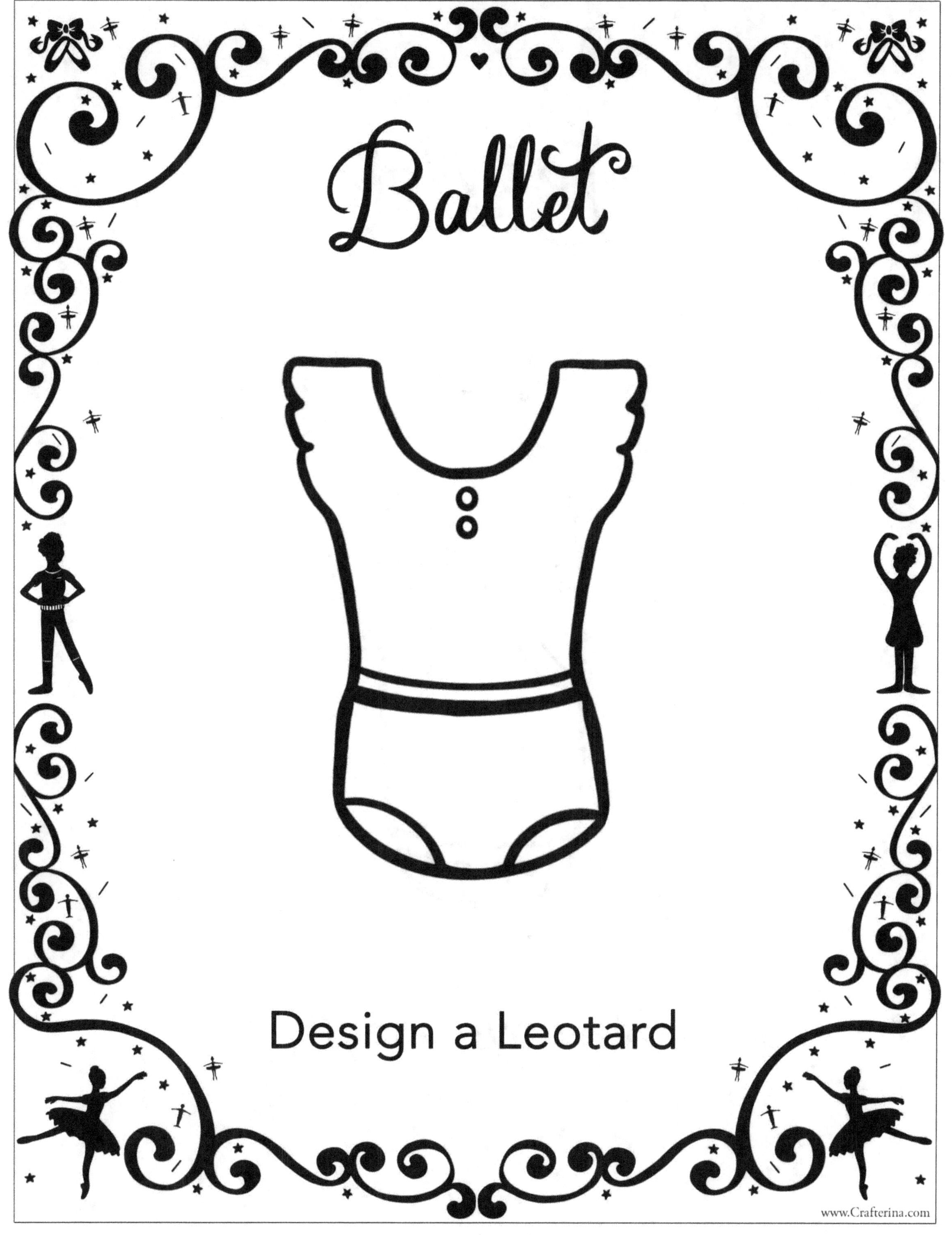

Ballet
Design a Leotard
www.Crafterina.com

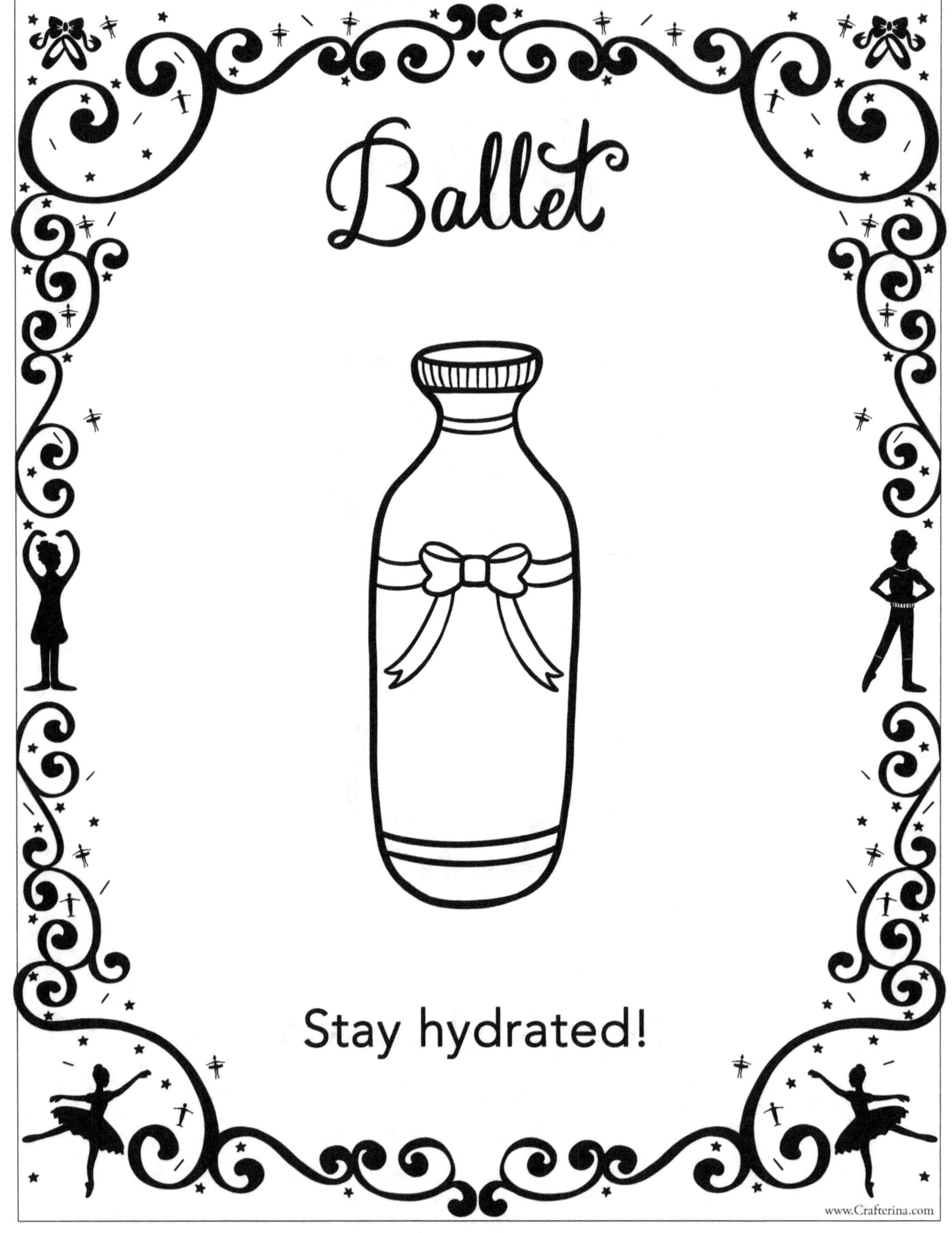

# Ballet

## Stay hydrated!

# Ballet

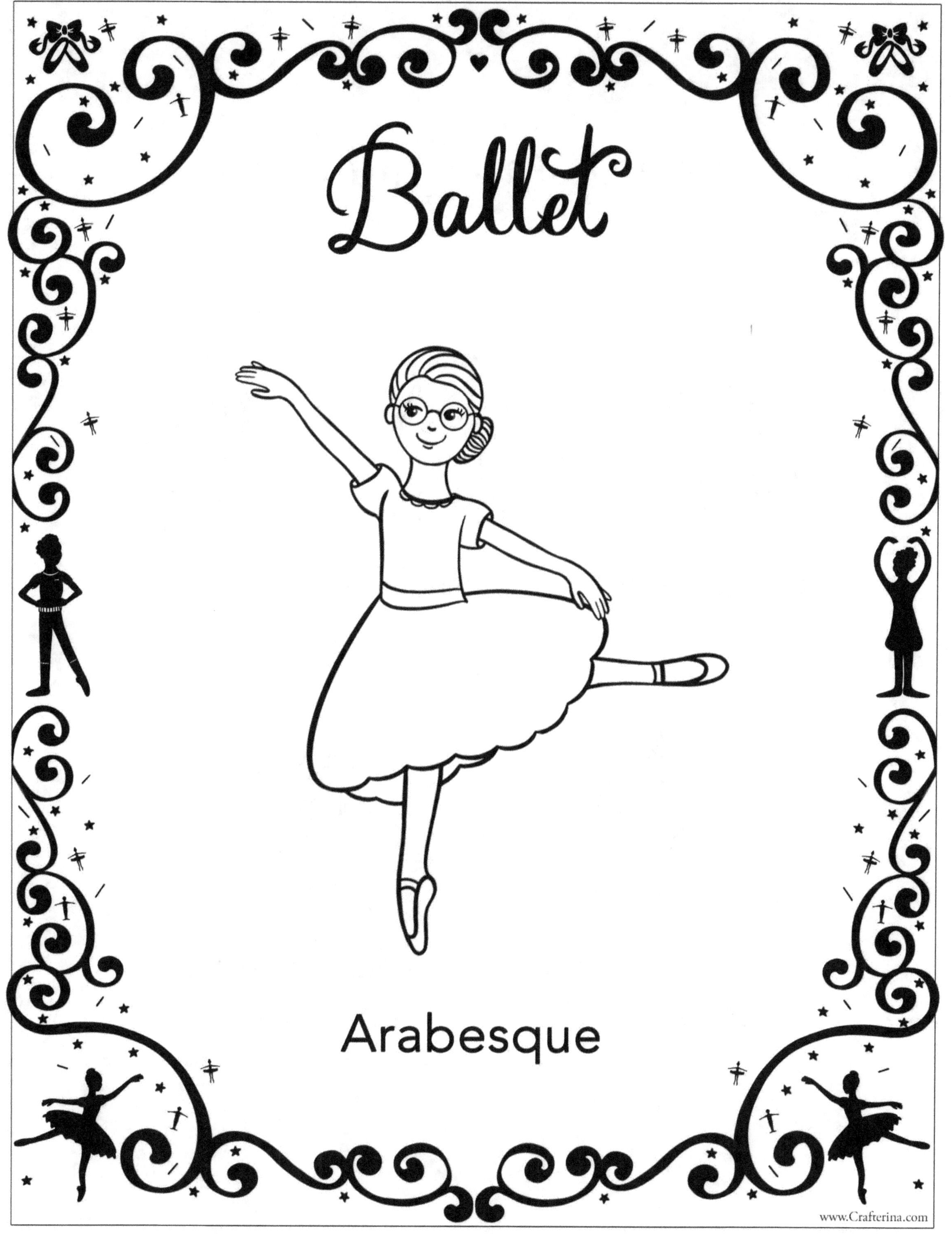

Arabesque

# How to Make a *Ballet* Bun

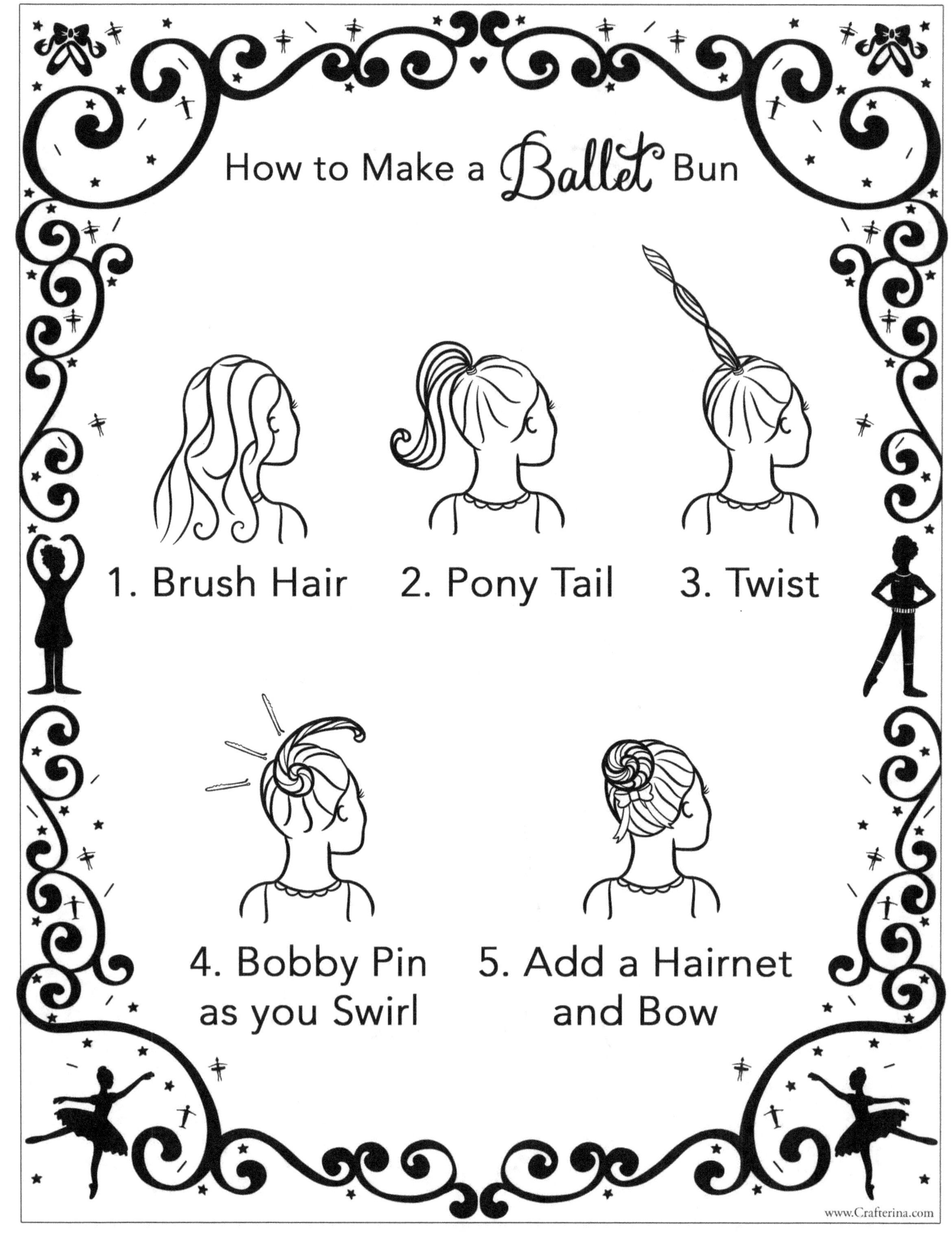

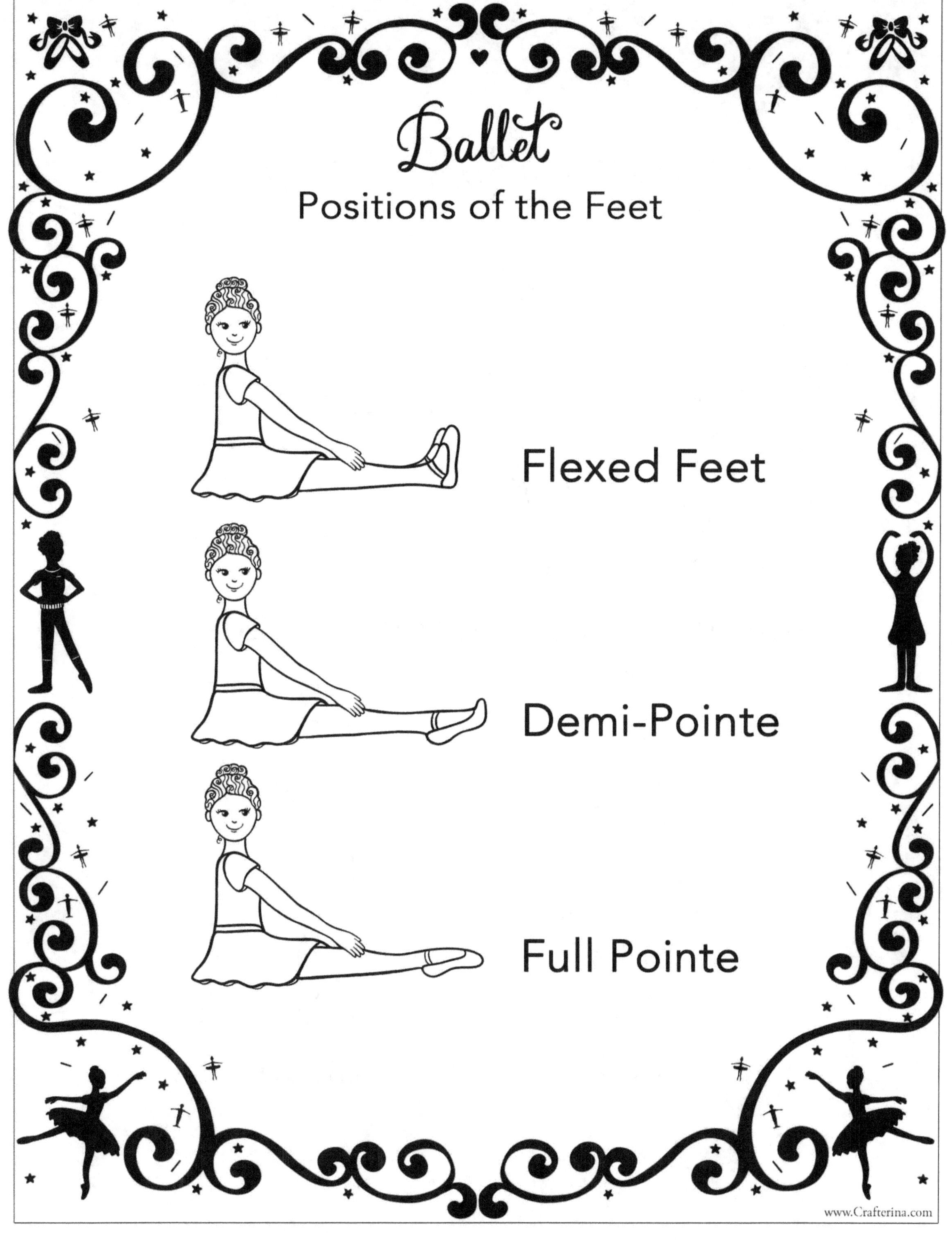

Ballet
Positions of the Feet
Flexed Feet
Demi-Pointe
Full Pointe
www.Crafterina.com

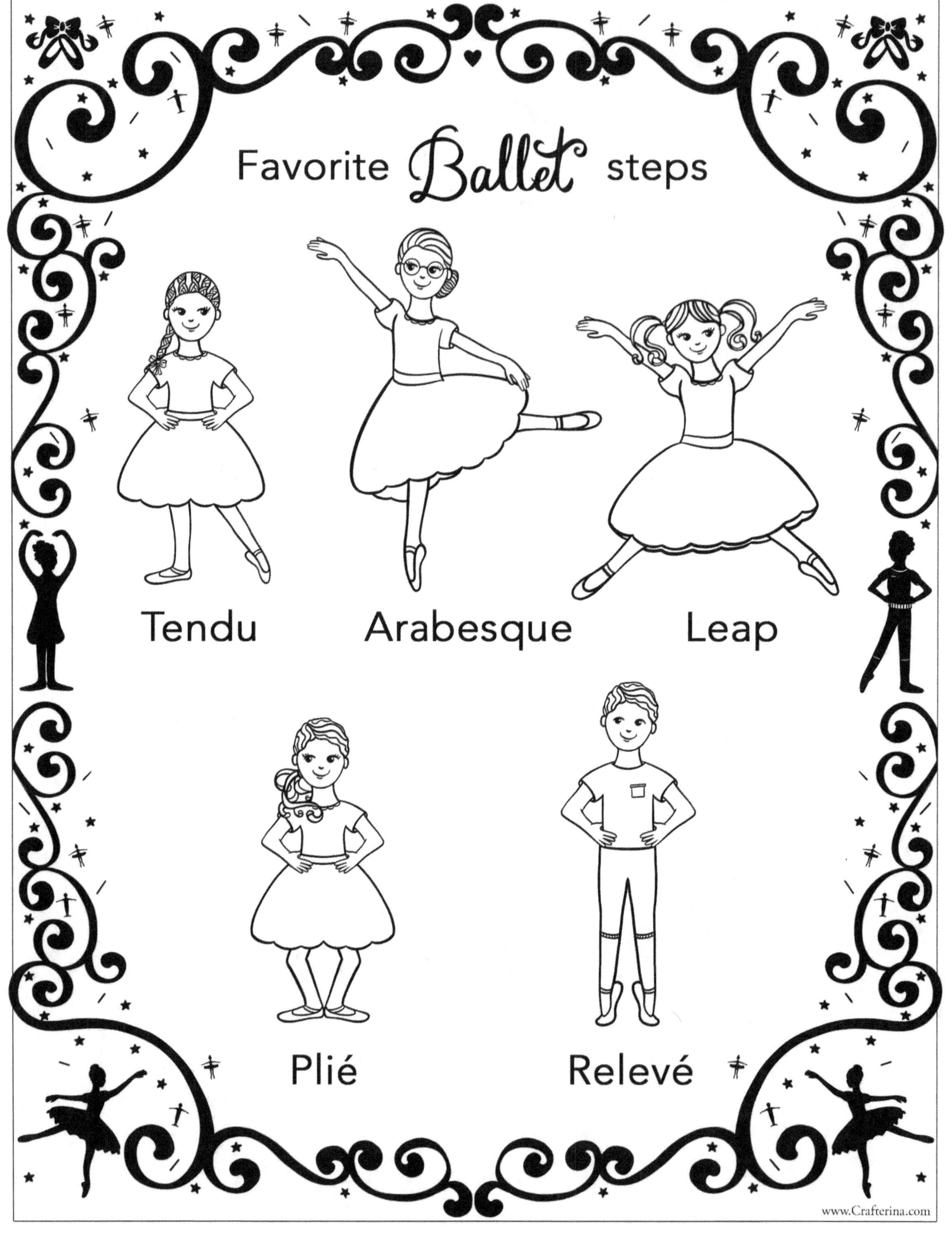

Favorite Ballet steps
Tendu
Arabesque
Leap
Plié
Relevé
www.Crafterina.com

# Positions of *Ballet*

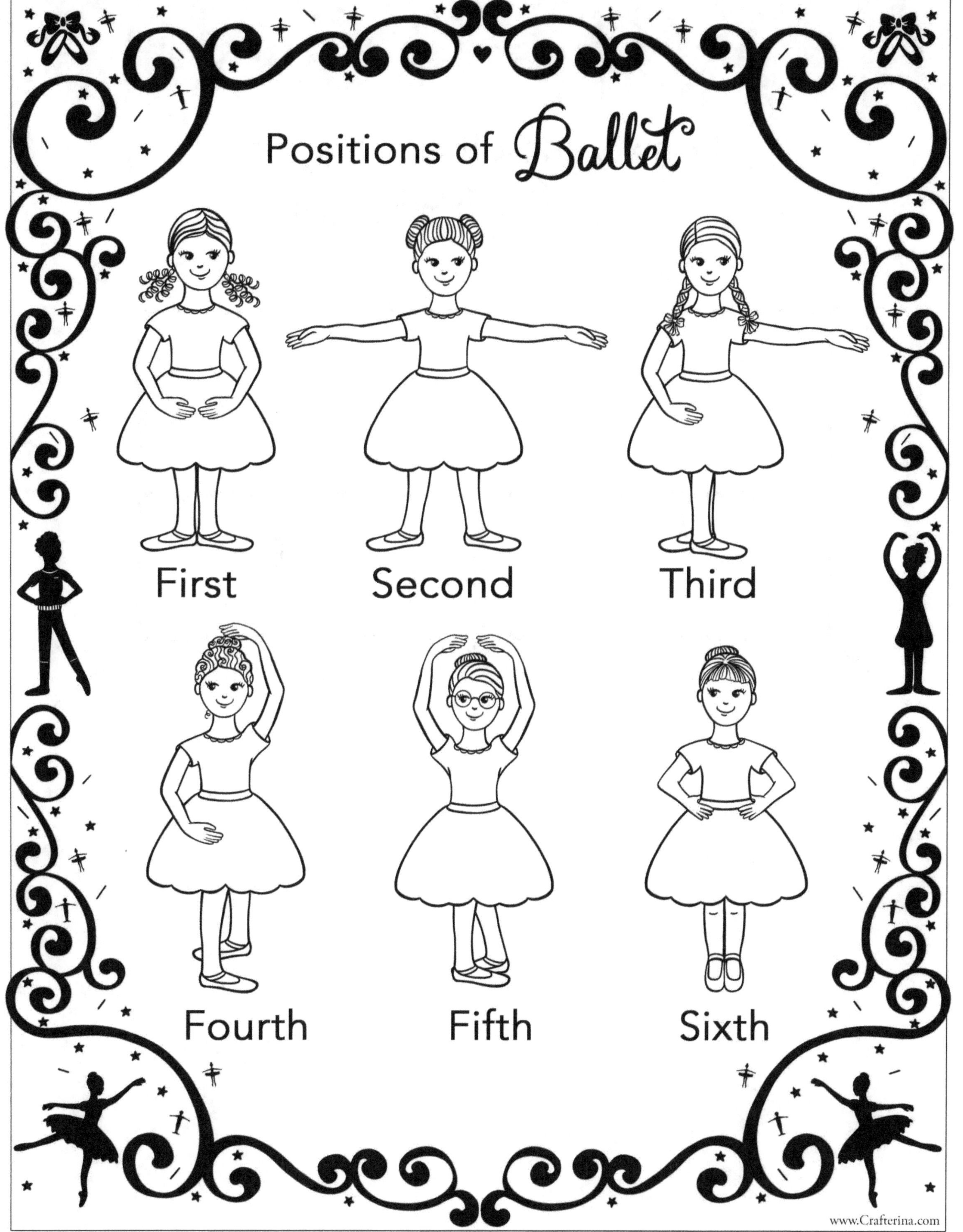

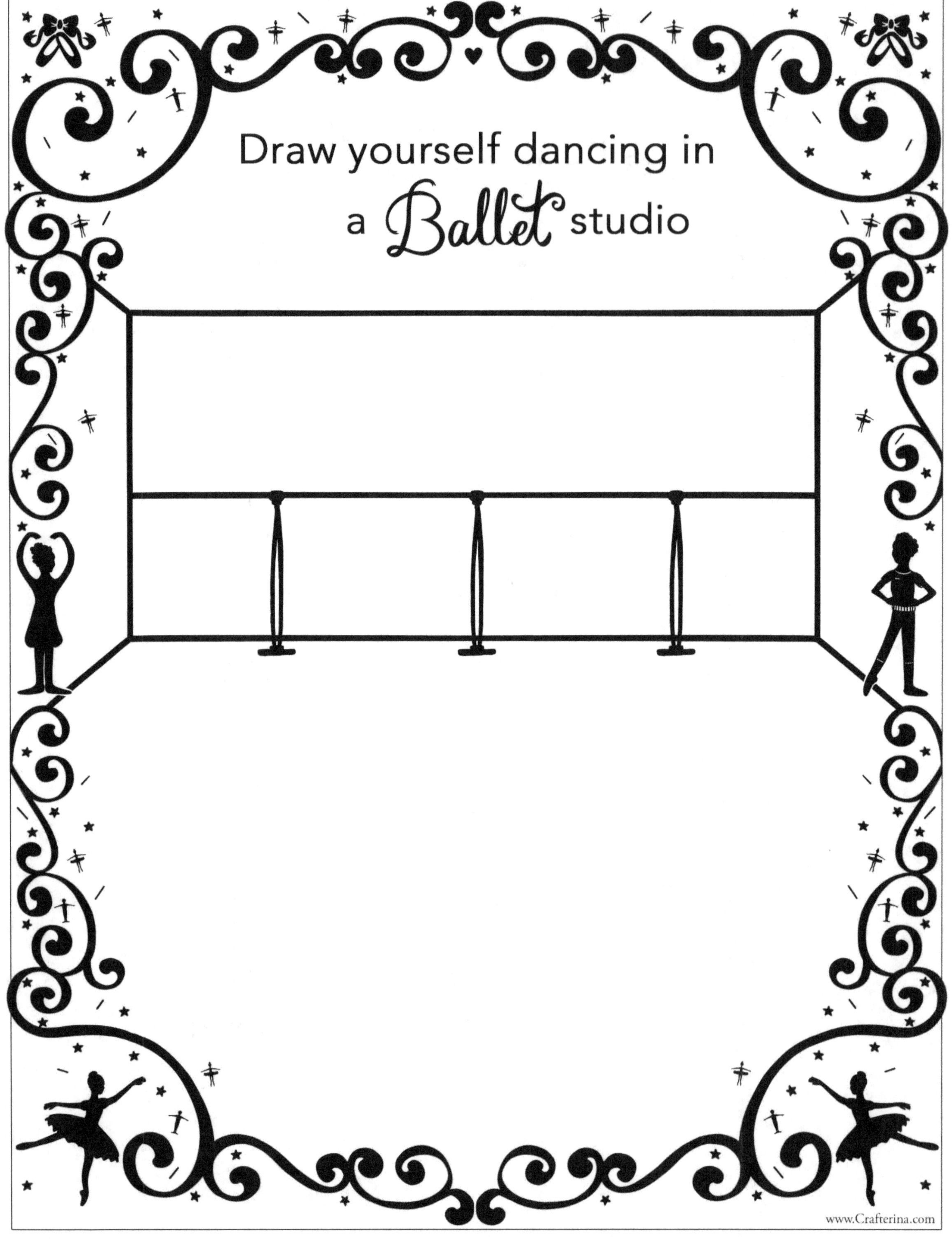

Draw yourself dancing in
a Ballet studio
www.Crafterina.com

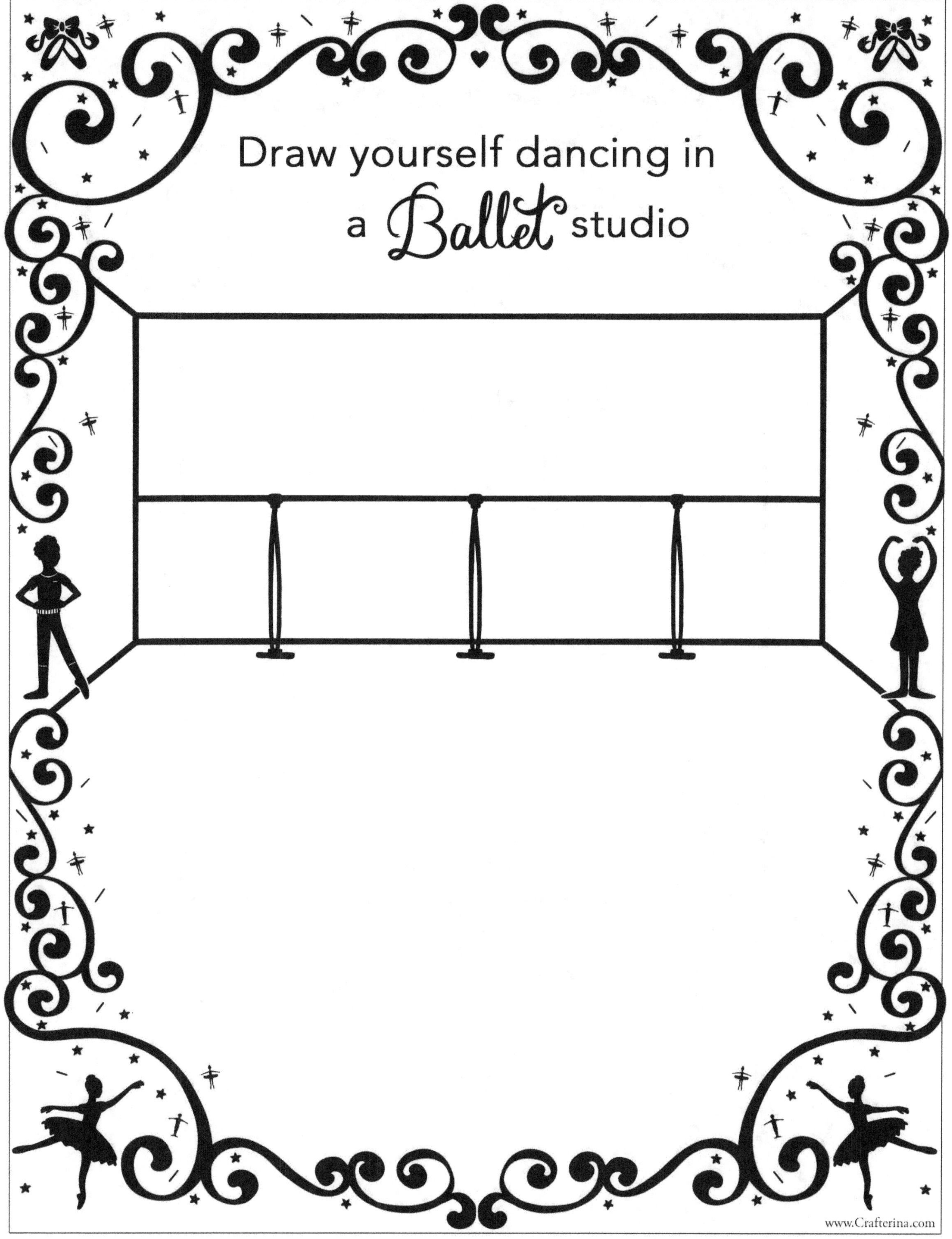
Draw yourself dancing in
a Ballet studio
www.Crafterina.com

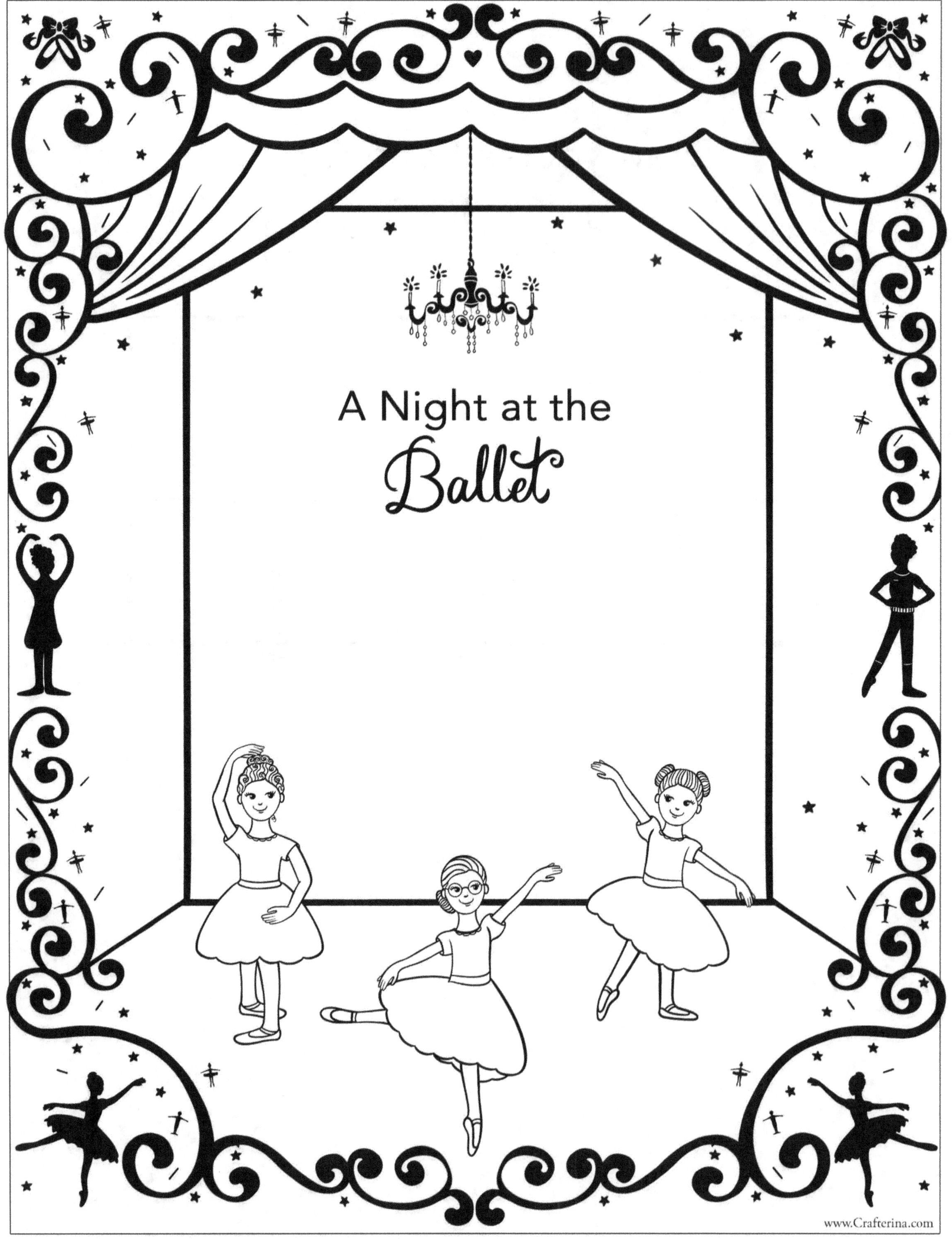

A Night at the
Ballet
www.Crafterina.com

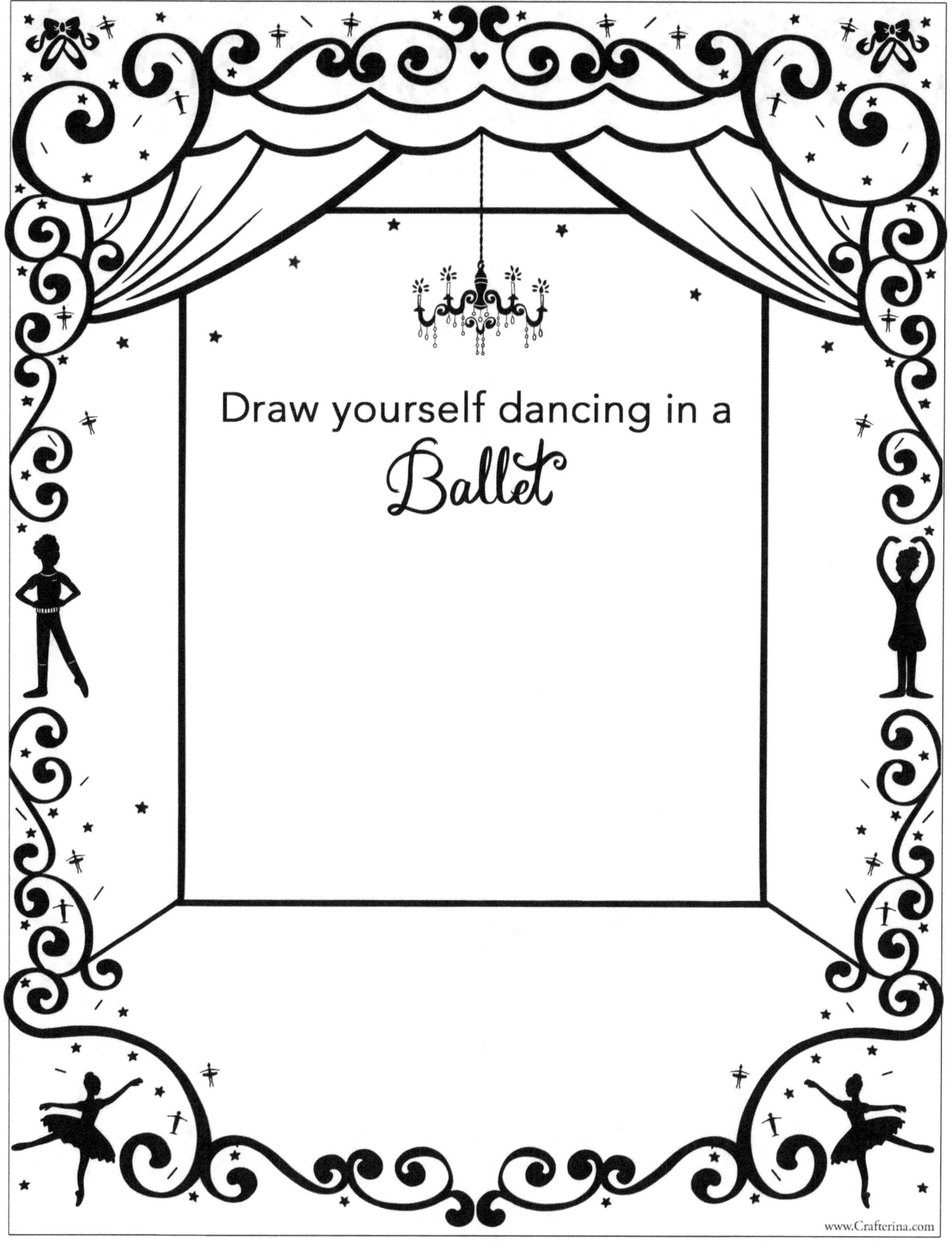

Draw yourself dancing in a
Ballet
www.Crafterina.com

# Ballet

## Draw the Other Half

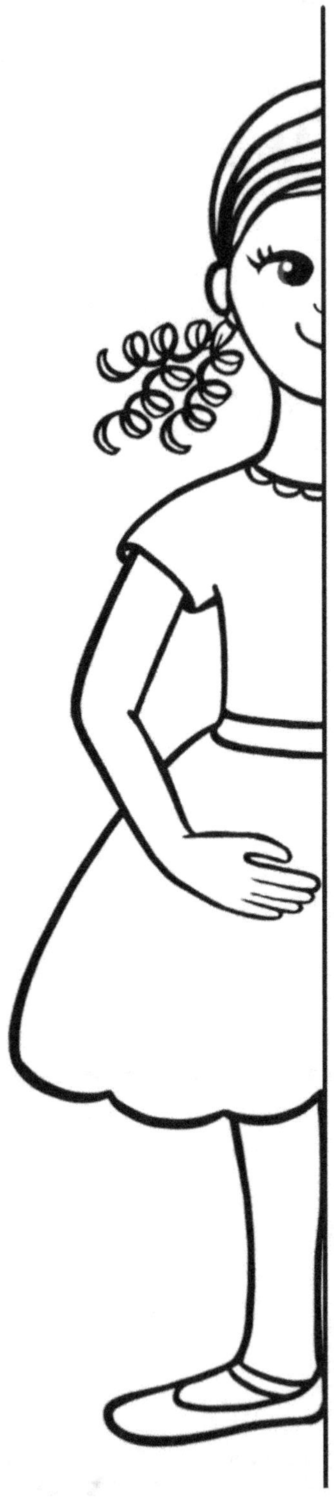

# Ballet

Matching Activity

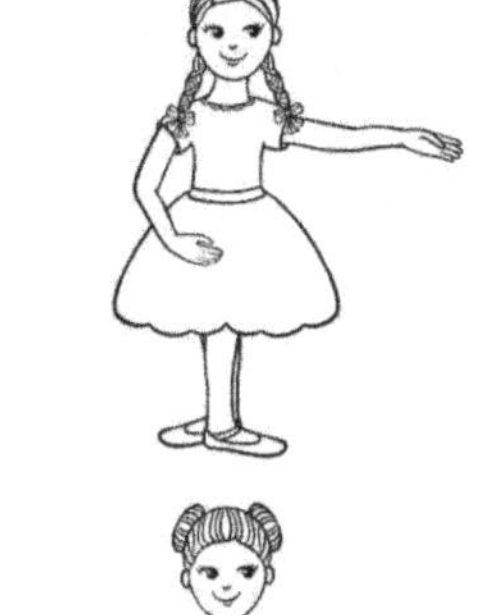

First Position

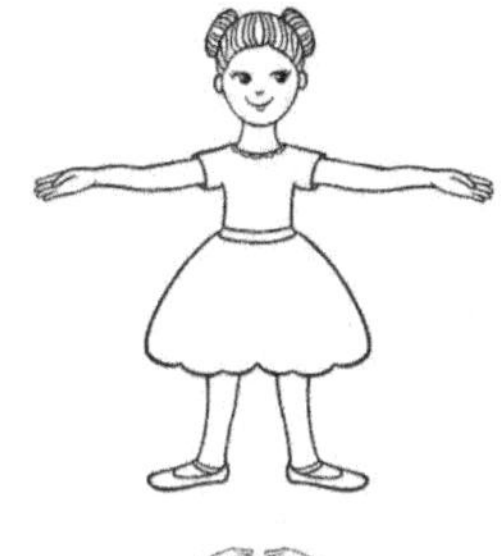

Sixth Position

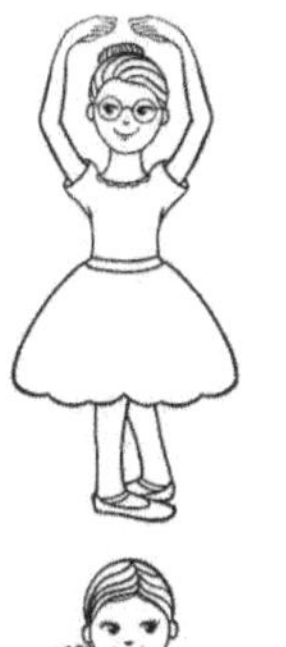

Second Position

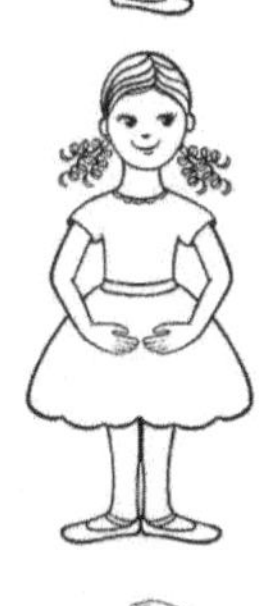

Third Position

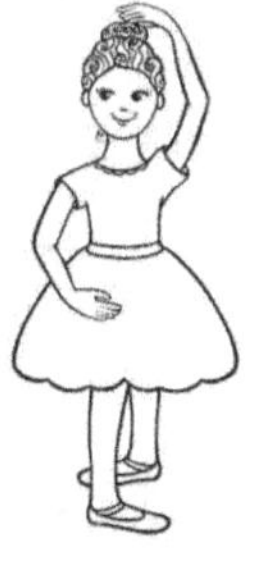

Fourth Position

Fifth Position

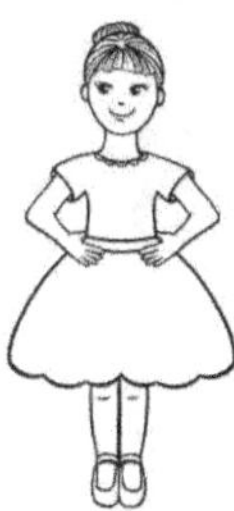

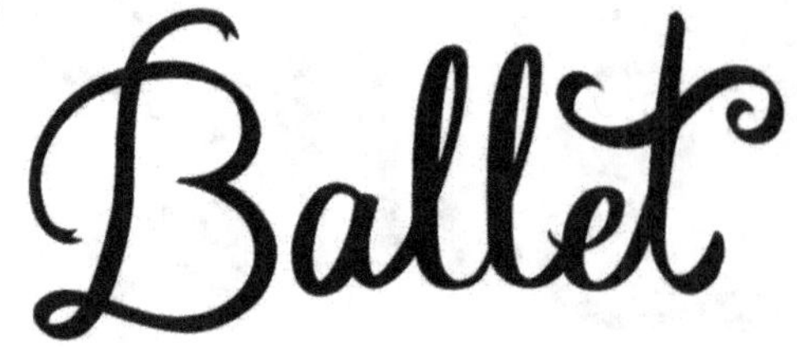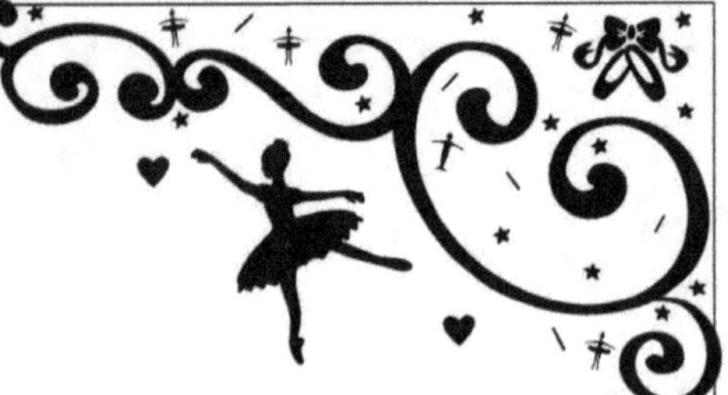

# Ballet

Connect the Dots Activity

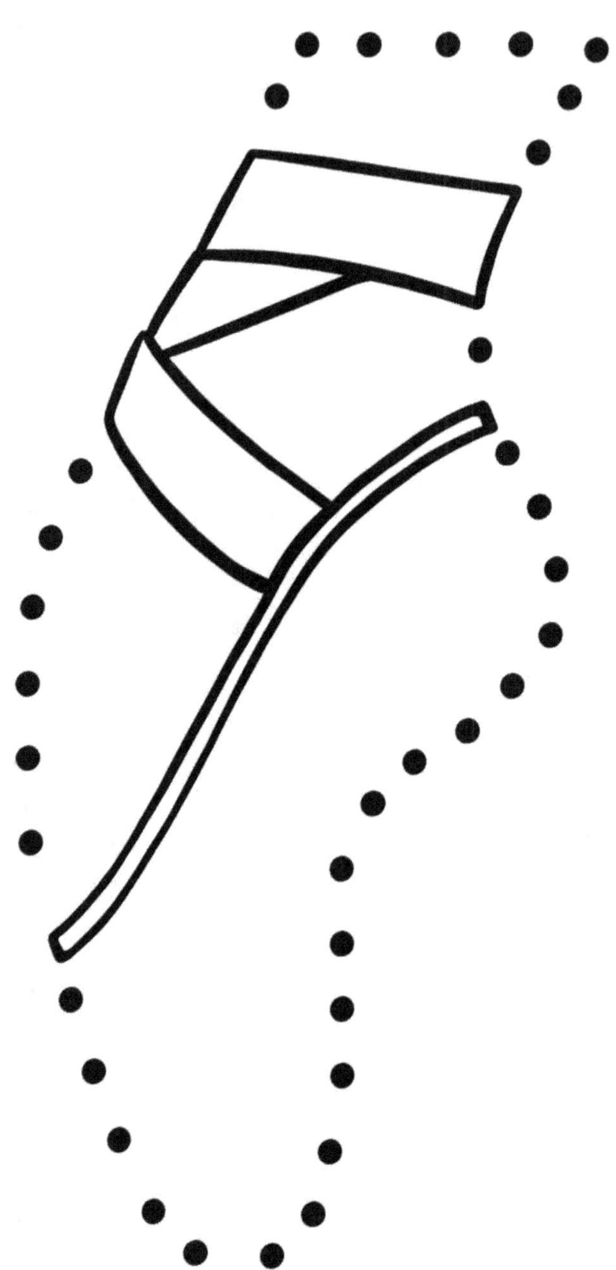

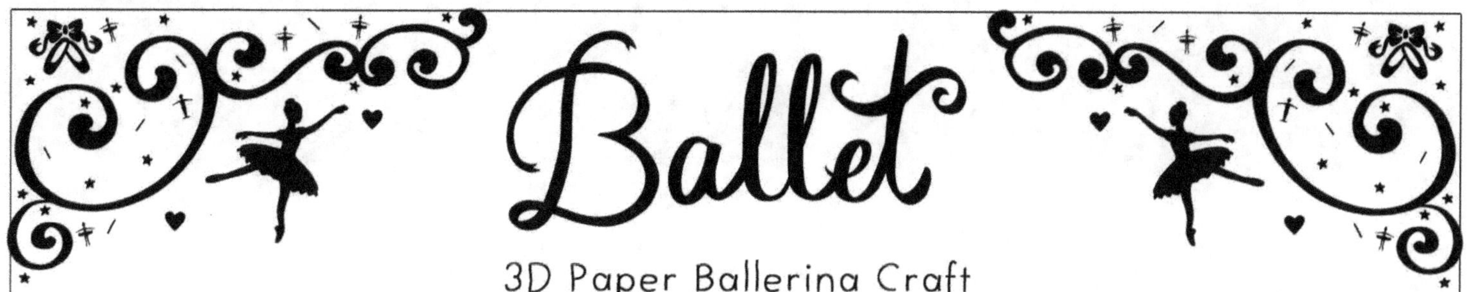


## 3D Paper Ballerina Craft

Safety Note For Parents: All crafts require parent supervision to create.
There are pieces to cut out that will require your help. Have fun creating together!

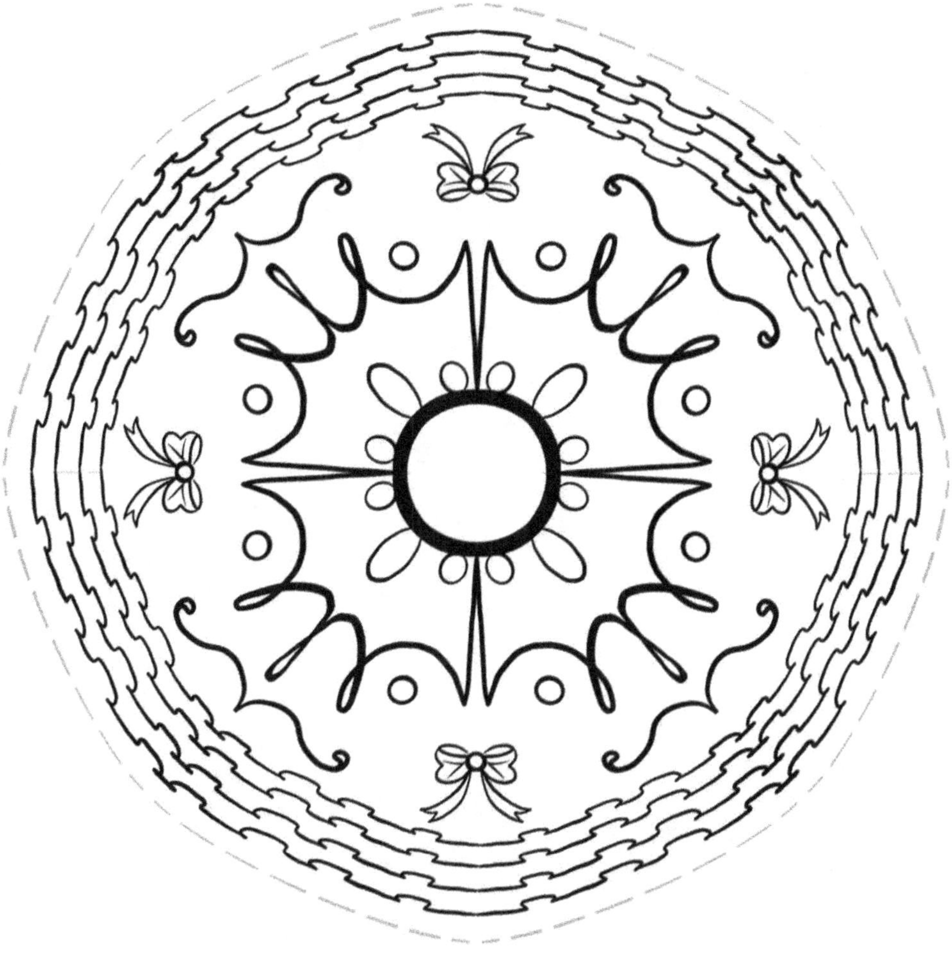

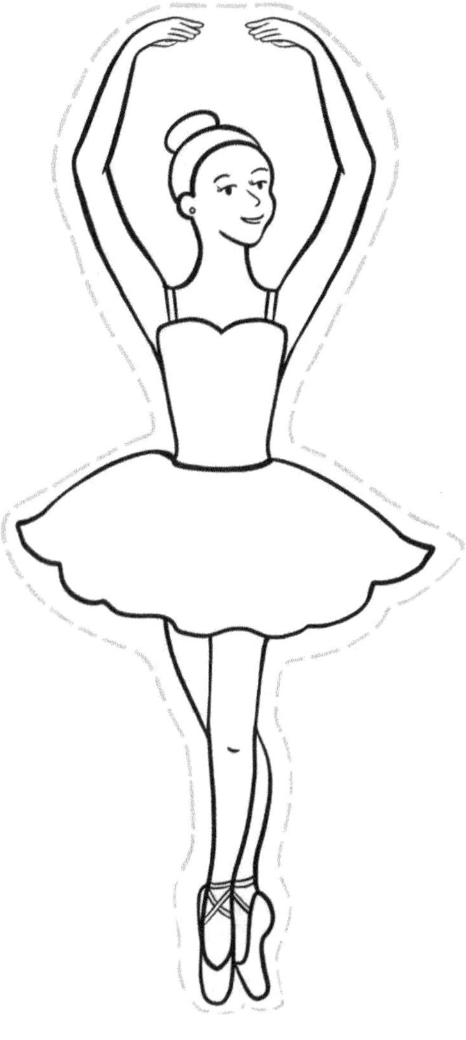

## Directions:

**1.** Cut out tutu and ballerina

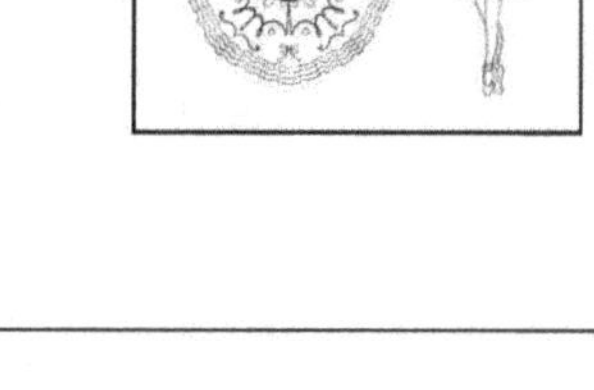

**2.** Fold tutu in half along dotted lines and cut out center circle

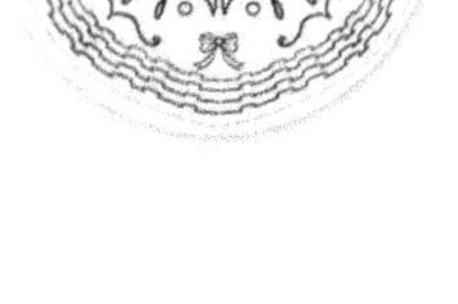

**3.** Gently bend to put tutu on

**4.** Place fold of tutu on ballerina skirt for stability

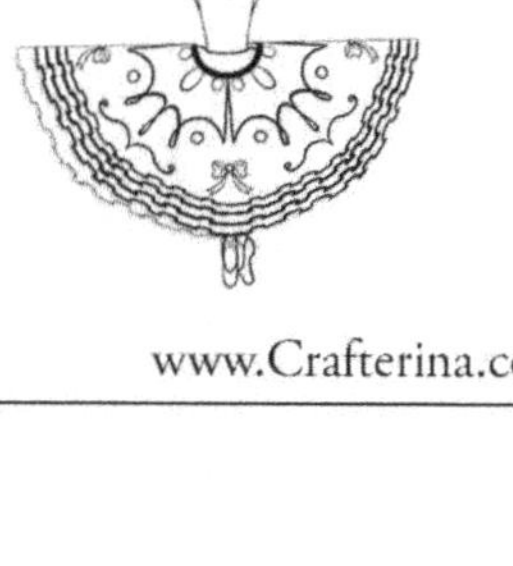

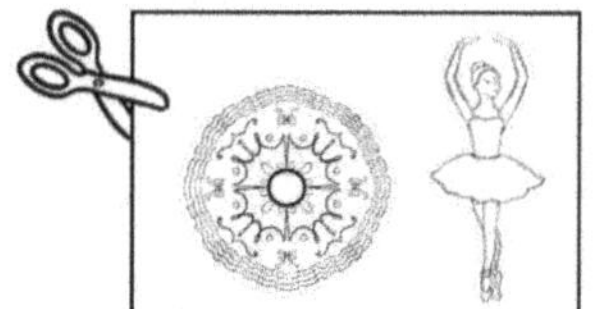
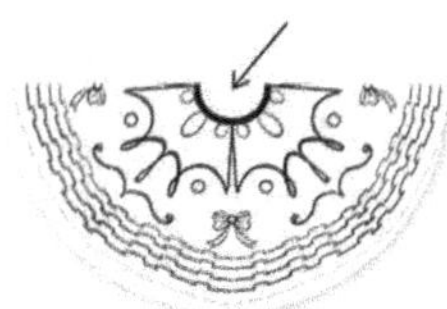
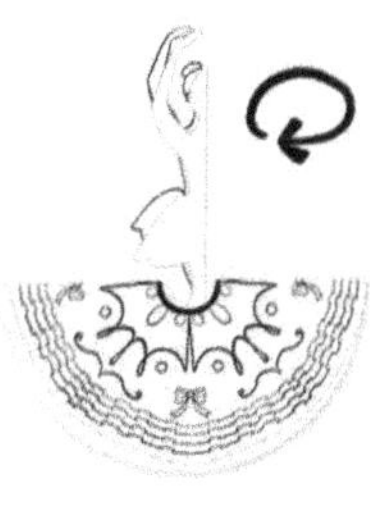
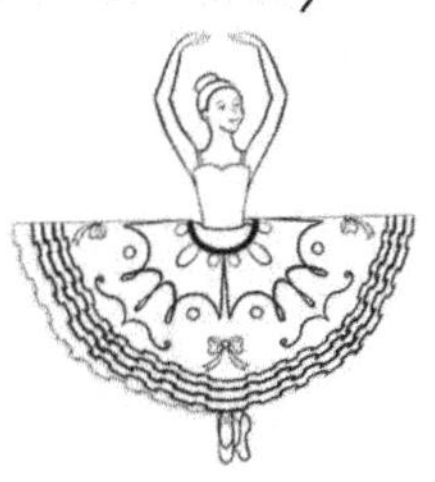

# Ballet

Ballerina Paper Doll Craft

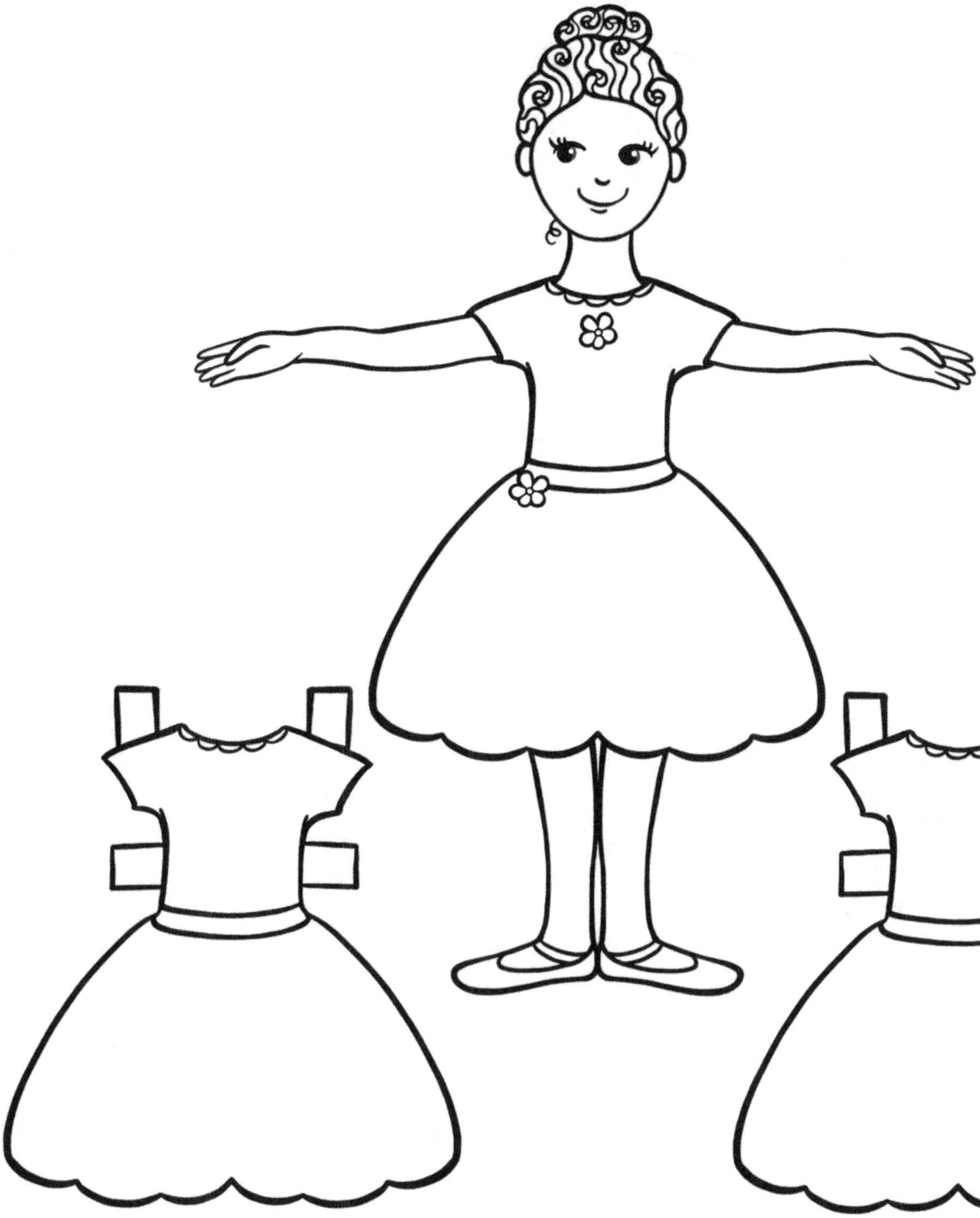

www.Crafterina.com

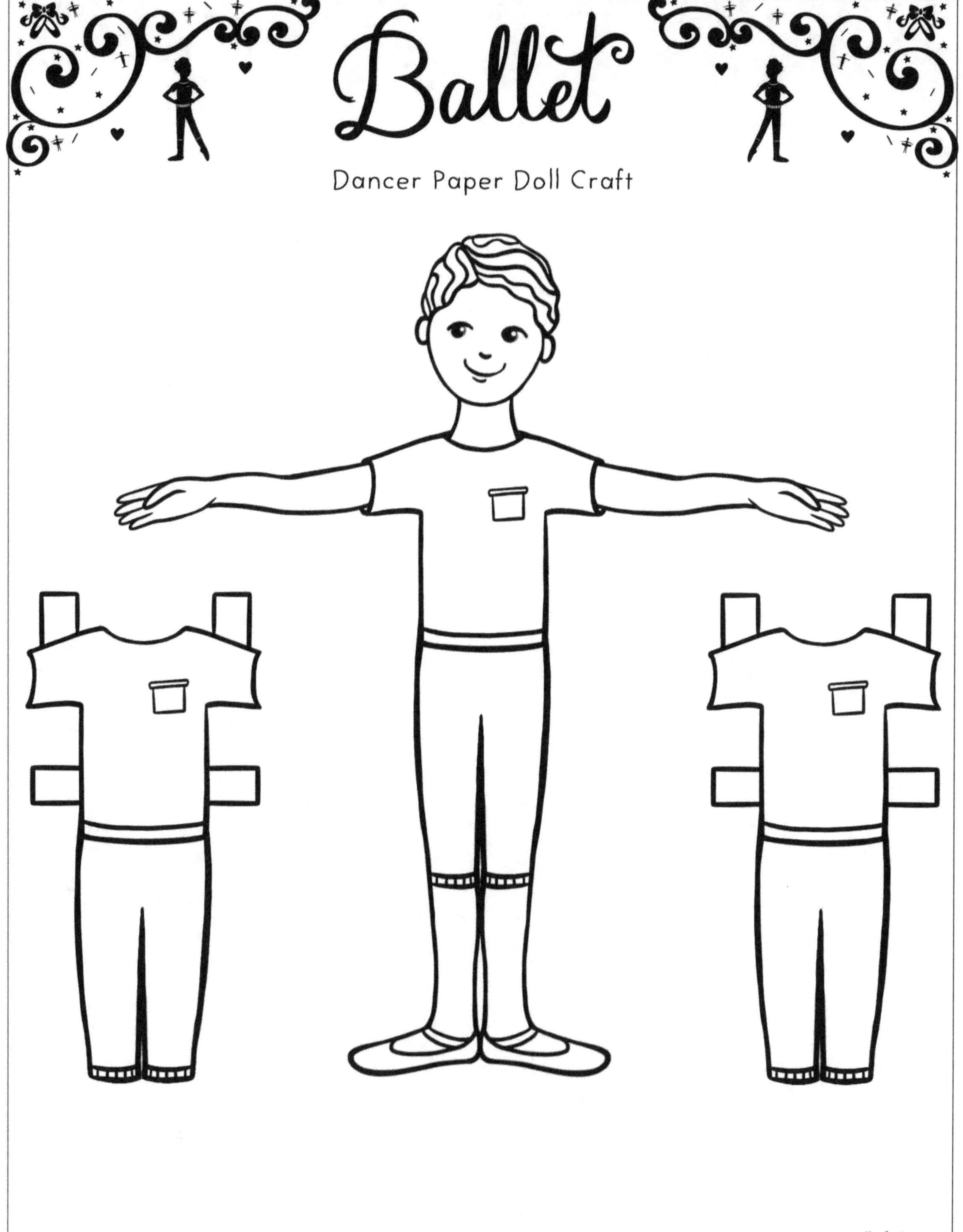
Ballet
Dancer Paper Doll Craft
www.Crafterina.com

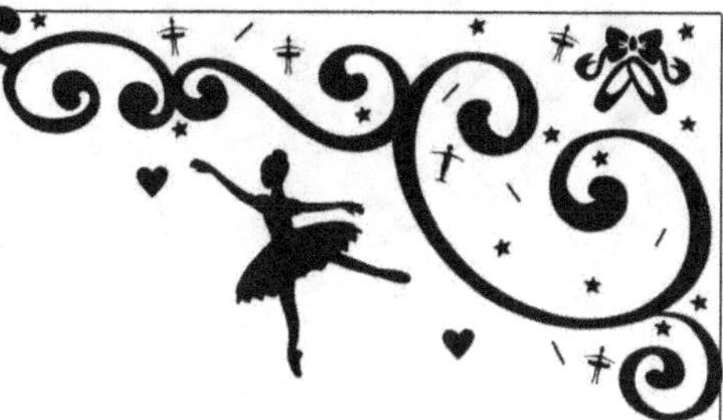

# Ballet

## Color & Create Puzzle

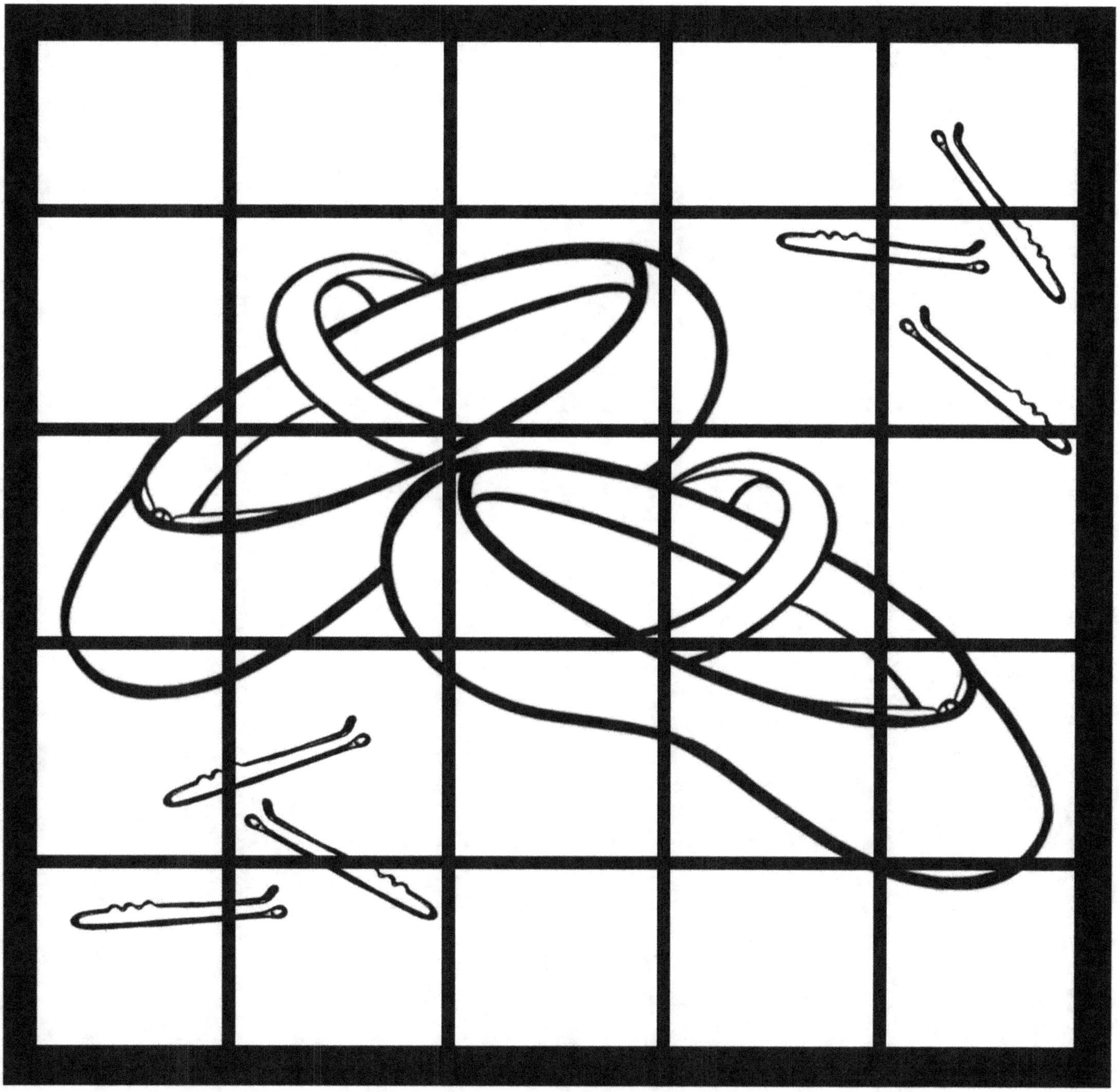

# *Ballet* Mask Craft Directions

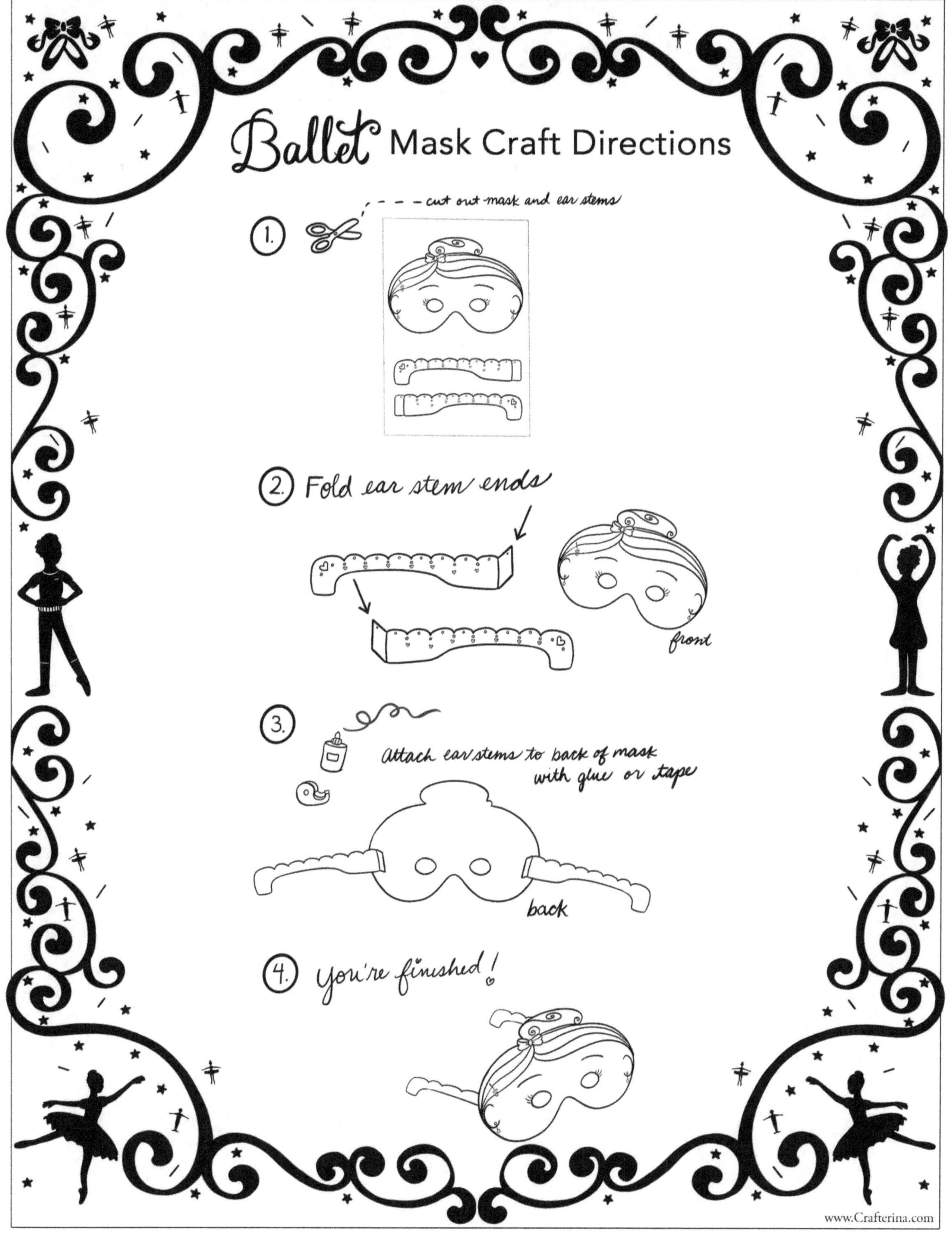

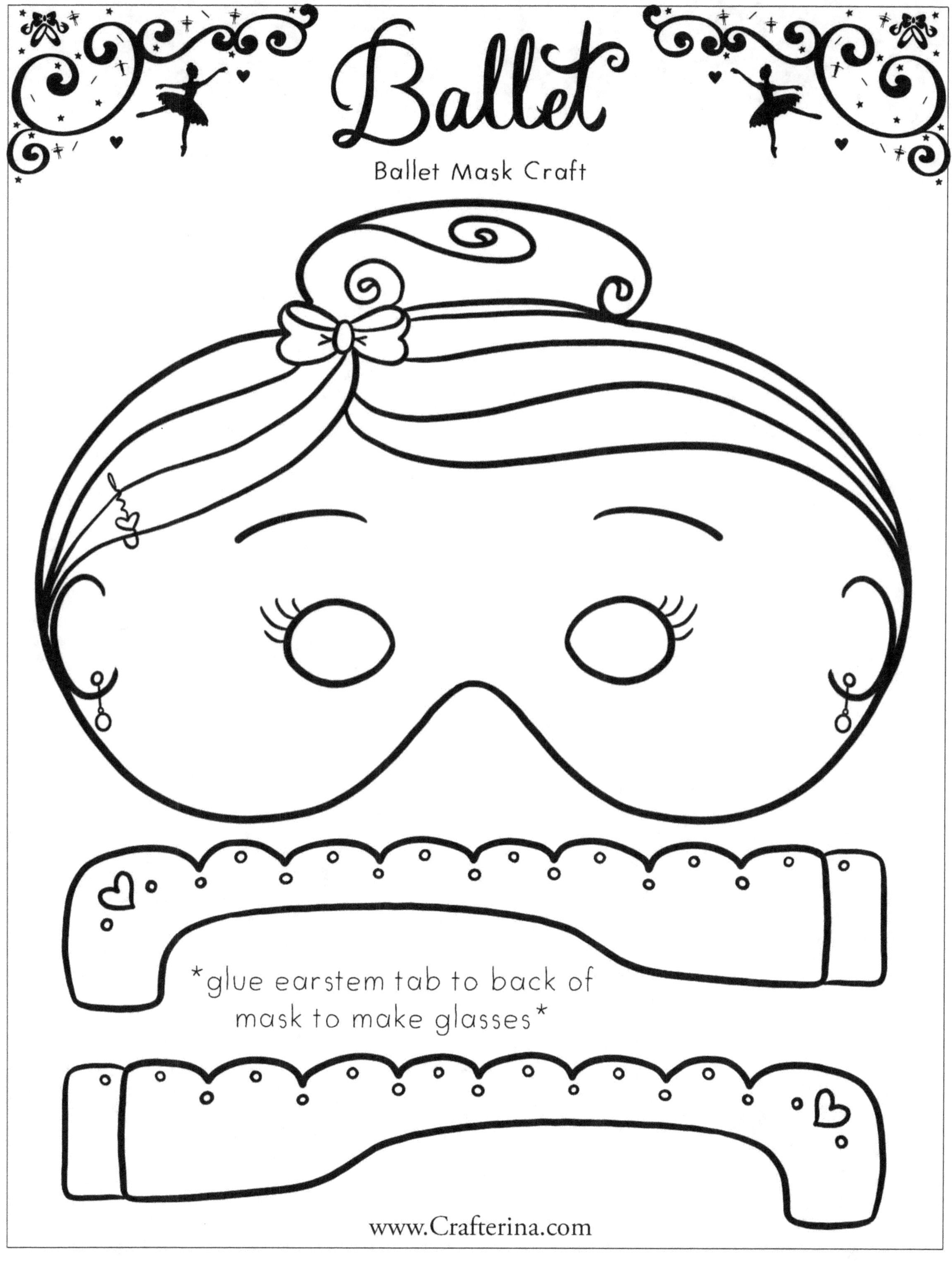

Ballet
Ballet Mask Craft
*glue earstem tab to back of
mask to make glasses*
www.Crafterina.com

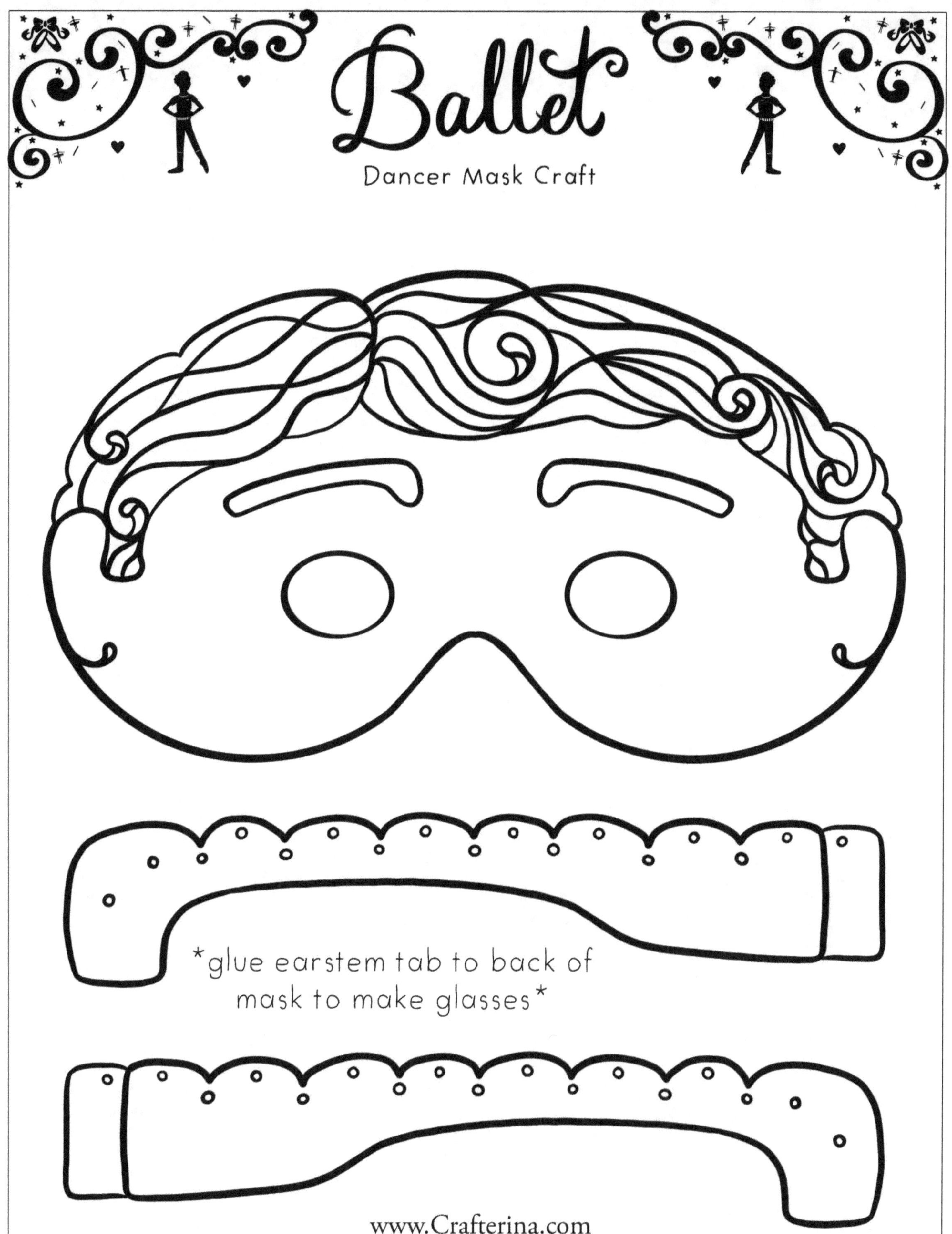

Ballet
Dancer Mask Craft
*glue earstem tab to back of
mask to make glasses*
www.Crafterina.com

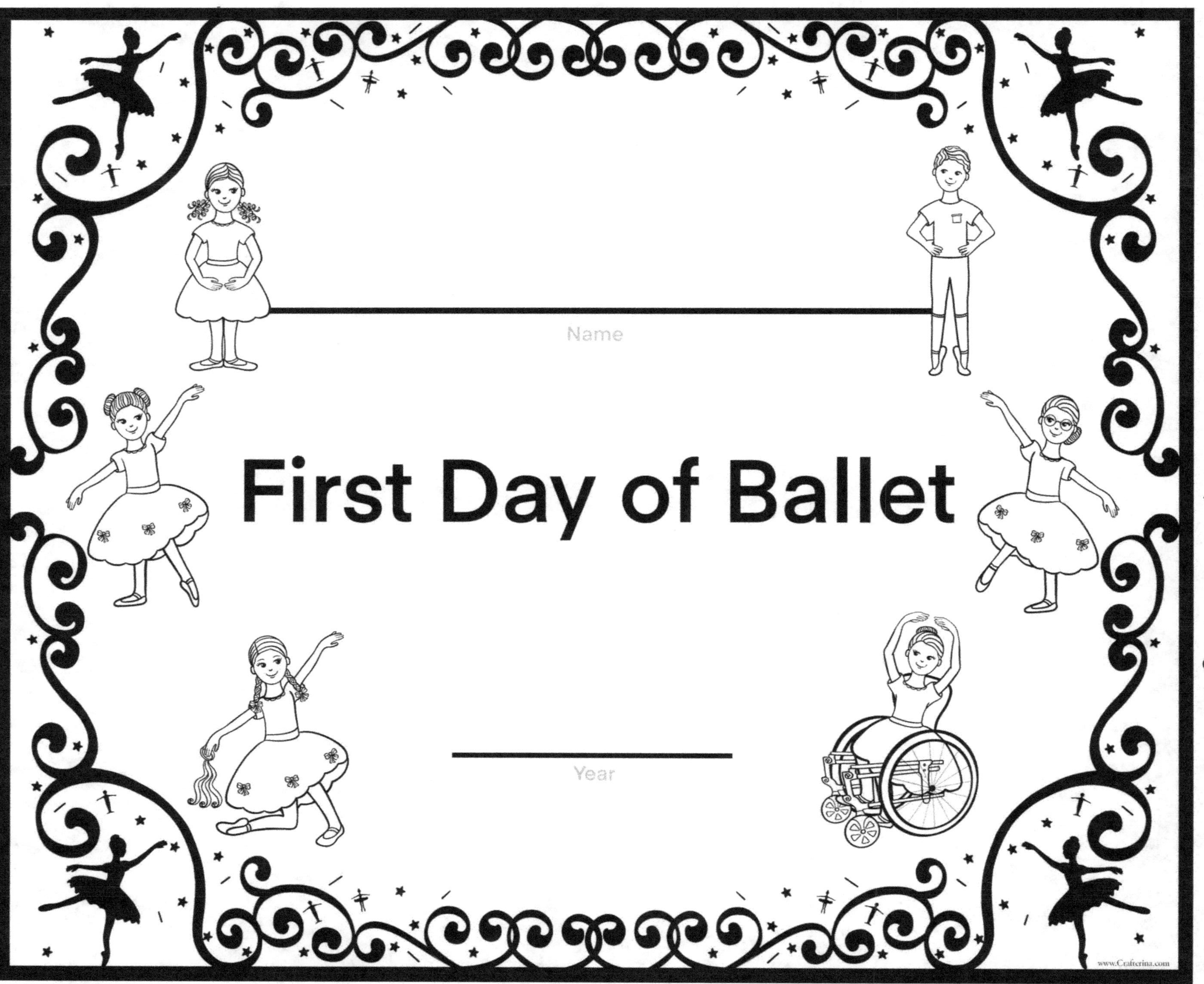
Name
First Day of Ballet
Year
www.Crafterina.com

# About the Author

Vanessa Salgado is a Professional Dancer, Educator and Illustrator.

She has taught many little dancers across Manhattan, concentrating primarily at the Joffrey Ballet School, School at STEPS on Broadway, and Alvin Ailey School. She has also worked as an Associate for the Education Department at New York City Center. Vanessa is a graduate of the Alvin Ailey/Fordham University BFA Program at Lincoln Center and holds a certification in Dance Education. Her work has been featured in Dance Teacher Magazine, Dance Spirit, Dance Informa, and METRO US Newspaper, among others.

Her earliest memories involve story time with her dad, creating with her mom after school, and attending weekend ballet class alongside her sister, Donna. Her interests in visual art revealed themselves wholeheartedly in high school as she simultaneously trained for the professional dance world. As she transitioned into her college days and into her professional life, her incessant doodles and crafting have remained a source of wonder for all those around her.

For more information:
www.VanessaSalgado.com

# About Crafterina®

Vanessa is also the creator of Crafterina® a series of dance education books and crafts for families. Designed to spark imagination and inspire movement at home, Crafterina® uniquely incorporates reading, creating and dancing in one. Through this interdisciplinary approach, Crafterina® playfully encourages empowerment and teaches youngsters they have the ability to make anything possible.

Inspire a lifelong love for learning in dance with the help of Crafterina®.

For more information, visit our website for books, crafts, and printables:

www.Crafterina.com

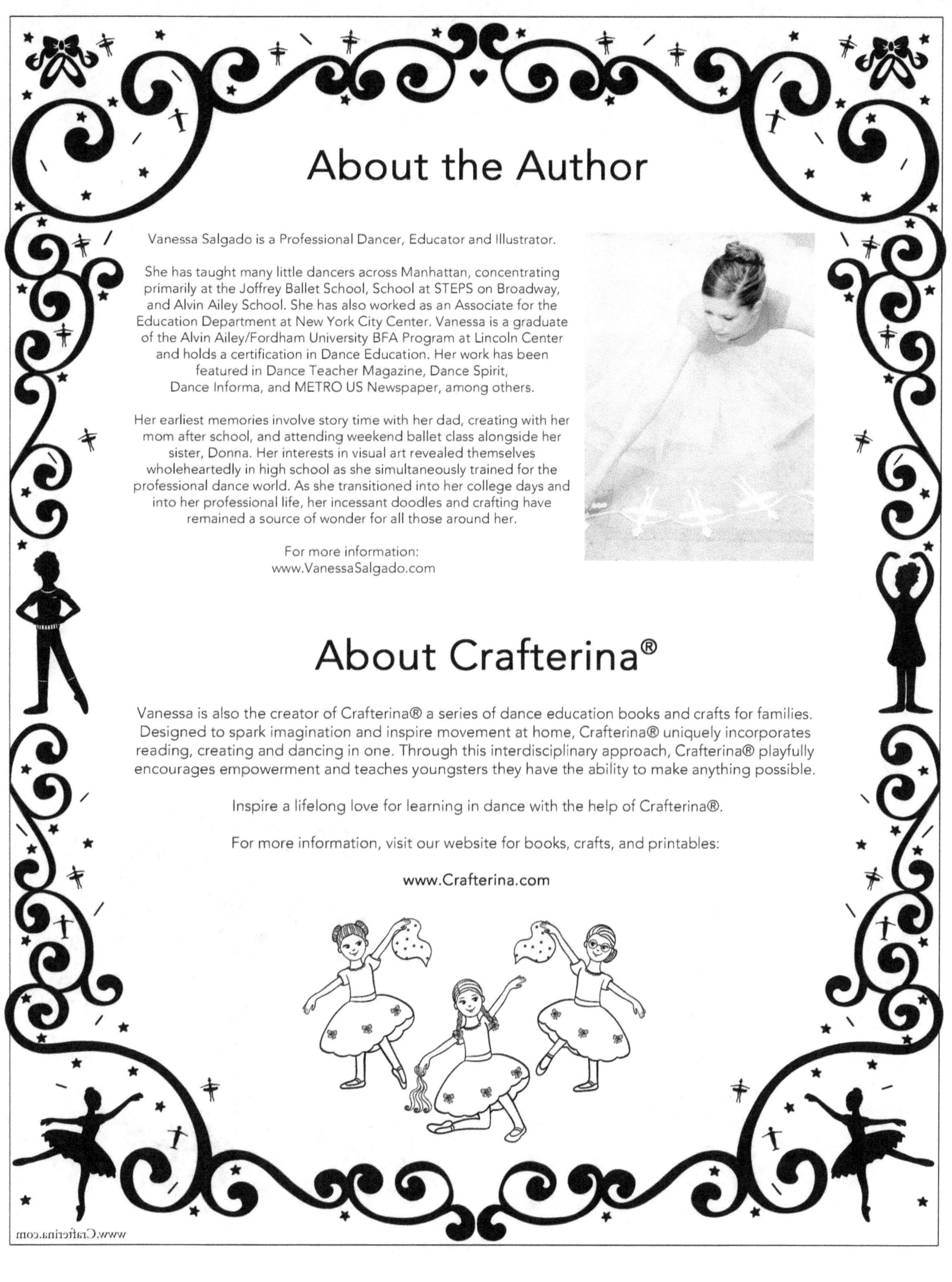

# Crafterina

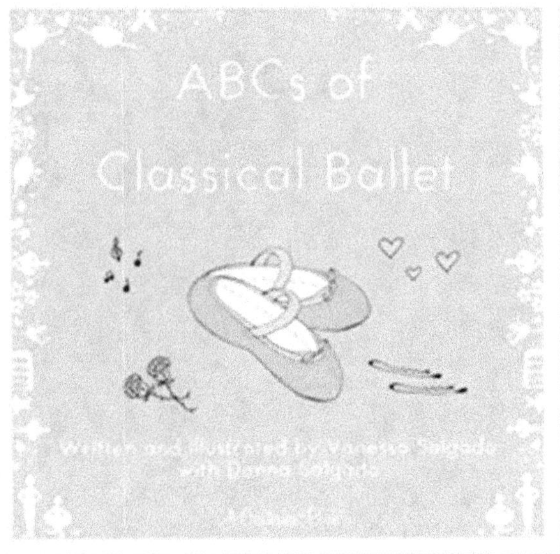

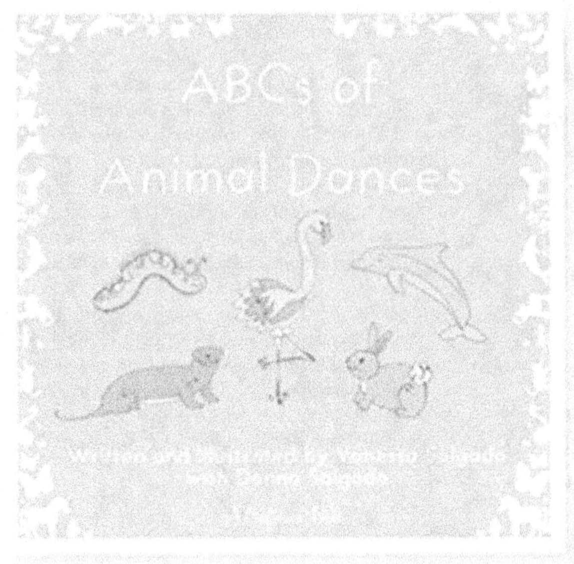

Find more from Crafterina by visiting our website:
www.Crafterina.com

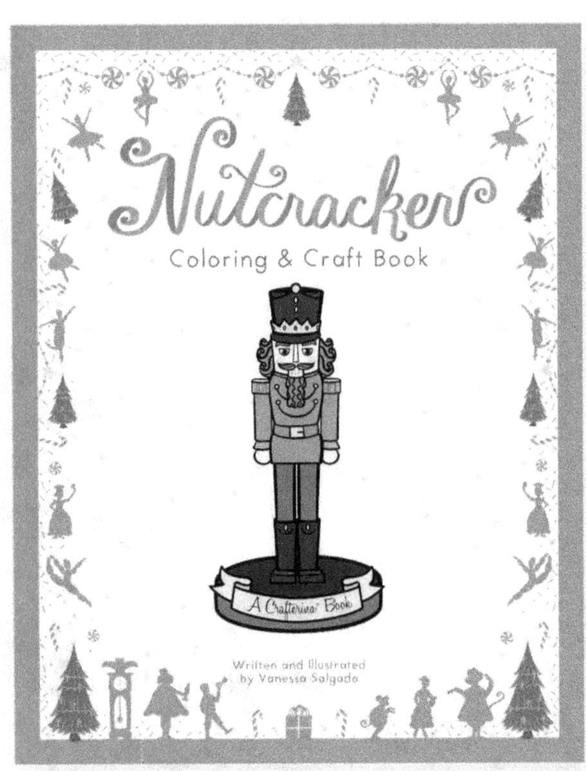

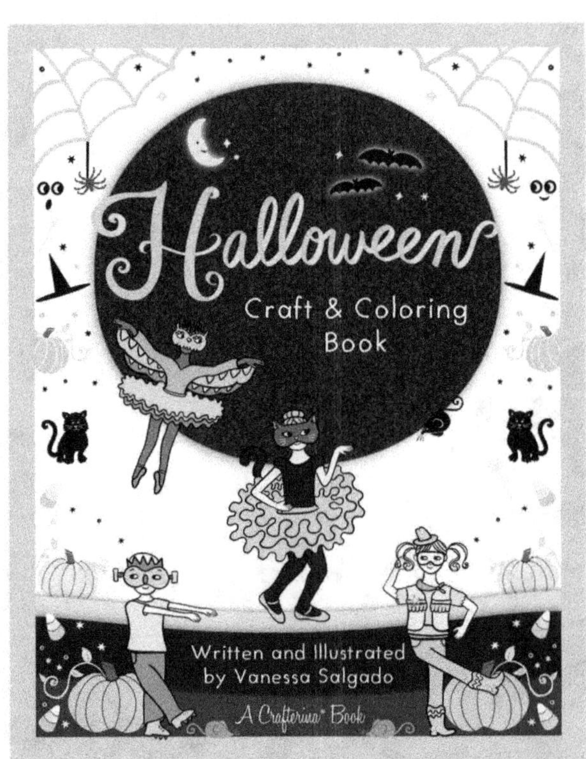